# A Pictorial Analysis of the Ramifications of the Concept of Boobieshandsstraps

**By**

**Professor
Vidanage P. Karunaratne**

# 01. Introduction

What is known as "Boobieshandsstraps? Generally, it denotes the universal practice of human females, irrespective of their age, colour, race or nationality and location, covering with one of their hands or both hands, the upper portion of their naked body (topless body) containing the pair of uncovered breasts demonstrating their shyness or bashfulness, especially if they happen to be in the company of predominantly males. The following pictures conspicuously illustrate this phenomenon:

(Incidentally, in reference to the three photographs depicted above, it must be obviously stated that prior to capturing this young beautiful curvaceous and voluptuous girl on camera with her boobieshandsstrap as planned beforehand, our discreet camera caught her in full nude rather unawares, at which point, feeling extremely bashful and shy, she abruptly put on her panties and covered her breasts with both her hands with their extended fingers.)

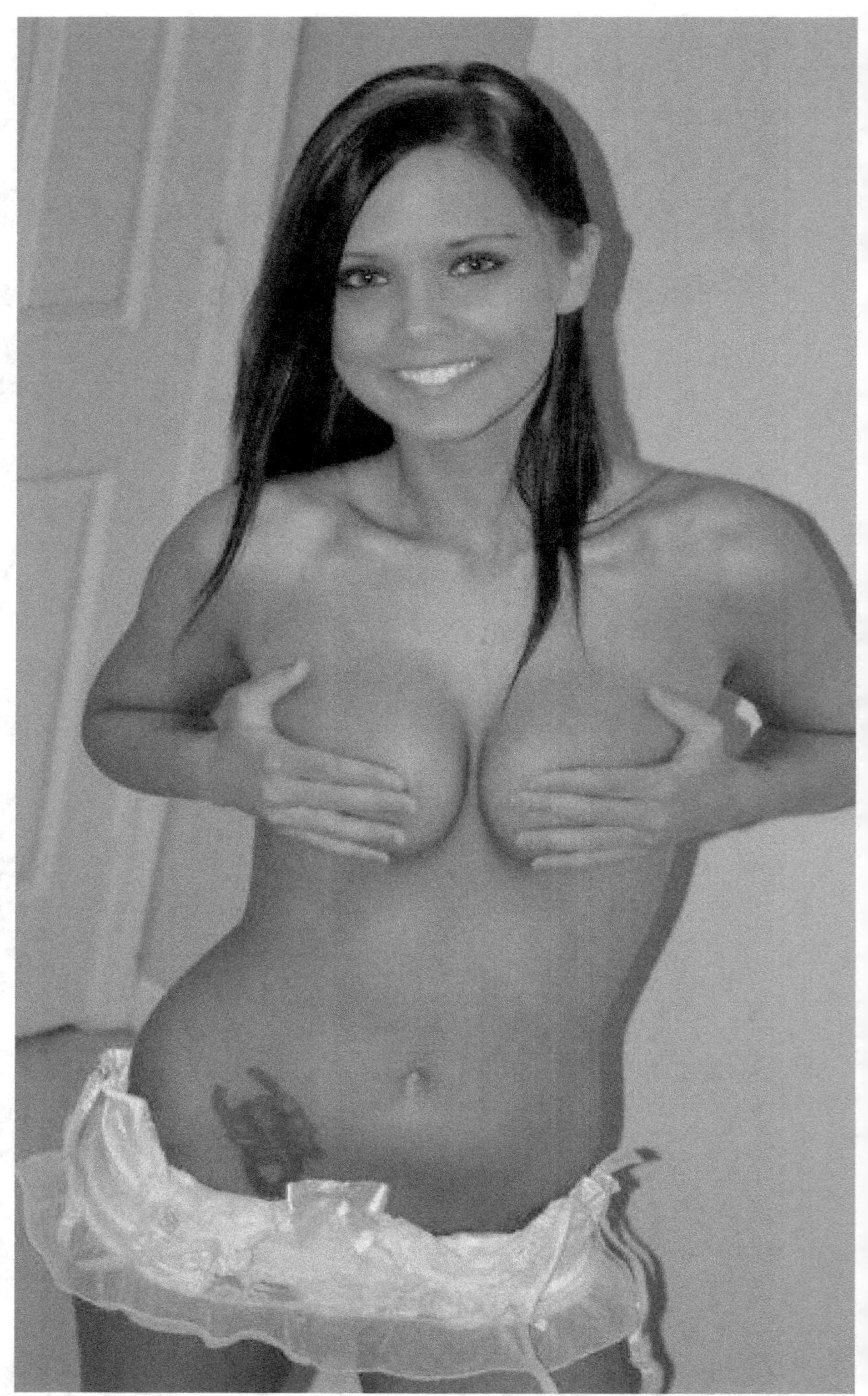

Thus, this pattern of boobieshandsstraps even applies to situations where females pose for photographs as models for various commercial products advertisements. Nevertheless, in situations where females are caught unawares when they relax topless, the natural and inevitable outcome emerging from them would be to abruptly cover their nude pair of breasts with their hands or arms, in other words, apply the theory and practice of 'boobieshandsstraps', whatever the circumstances would be. Therefore, while analysing this almost natural phenomenon, it appears like it is universal in nature, traits and

characteristics. Here are many more pictures to substantiate th
phenomenon:

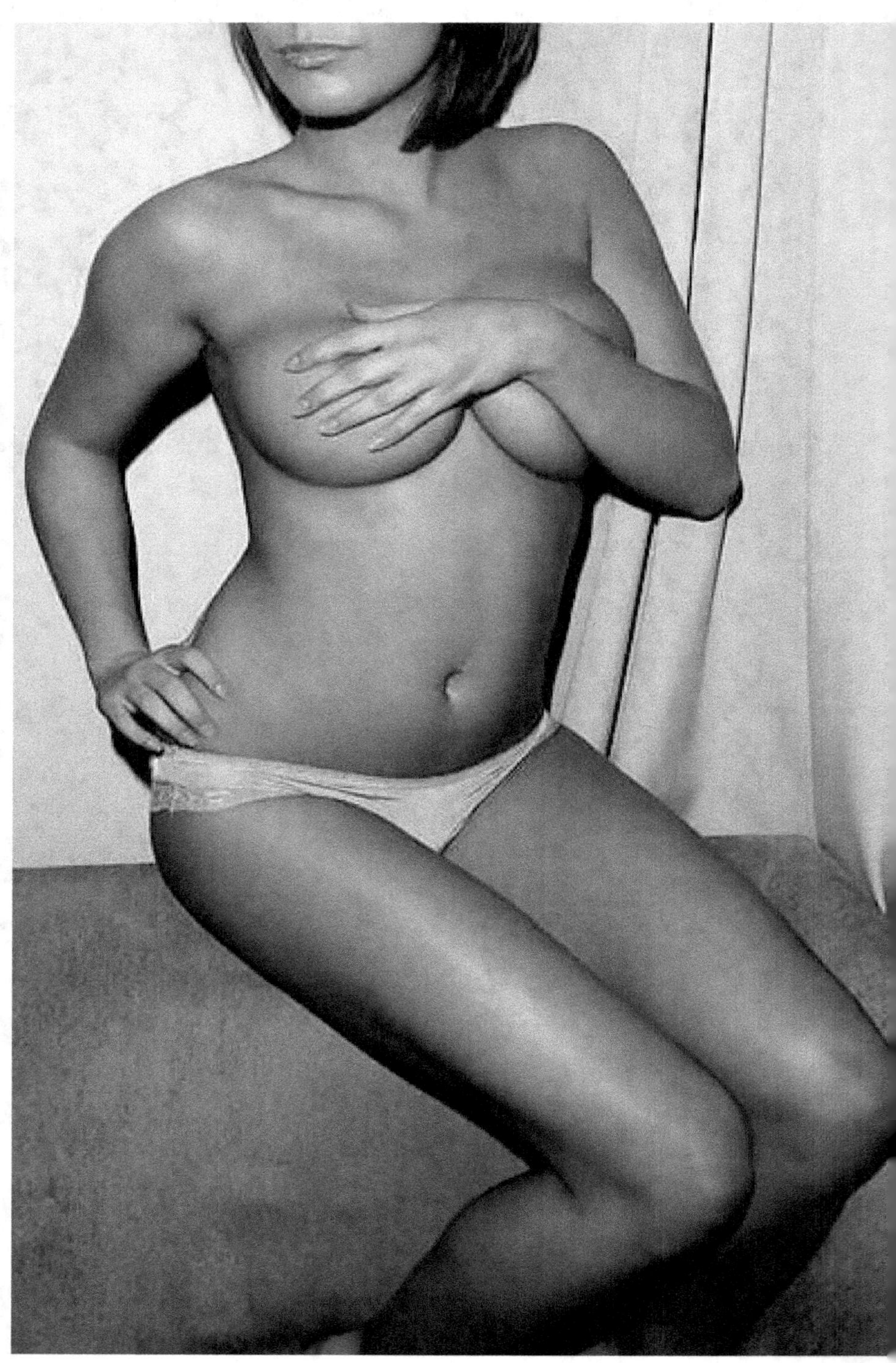

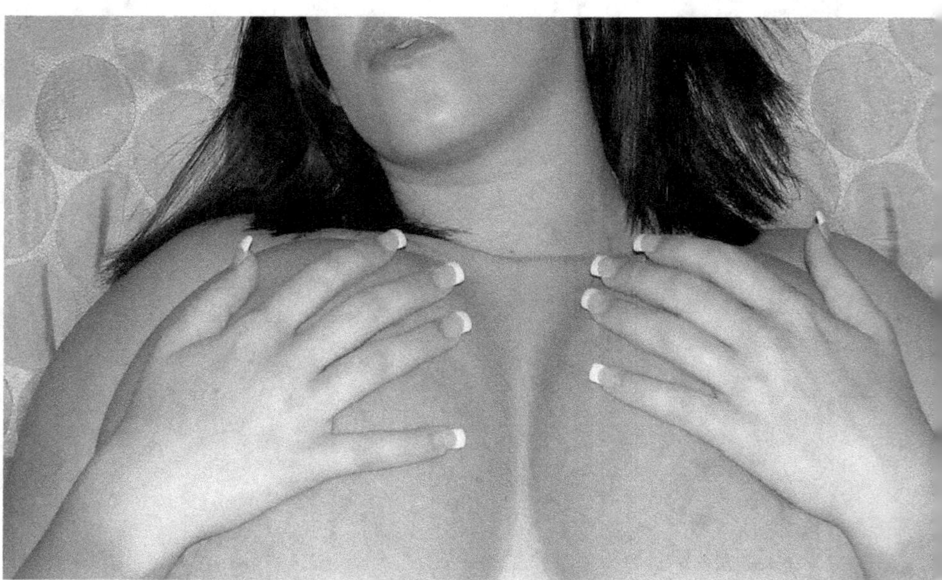

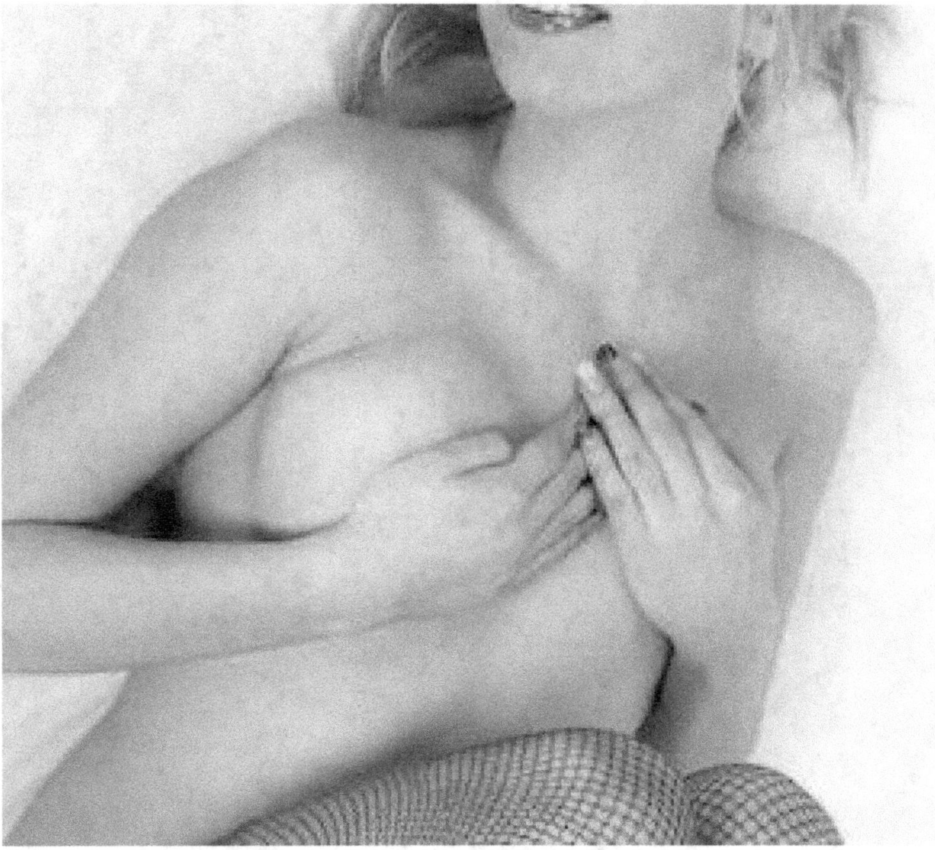

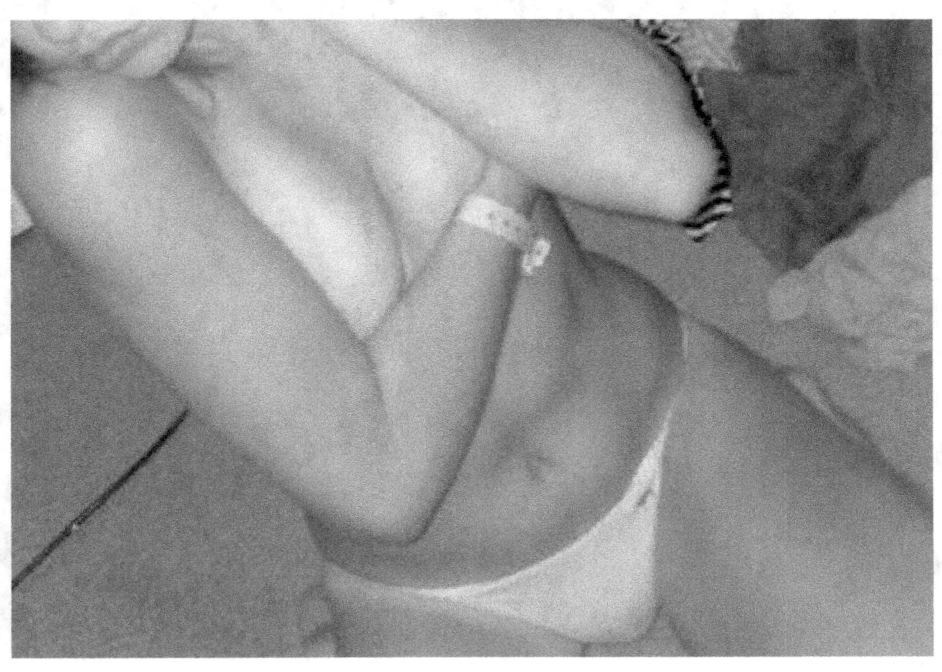

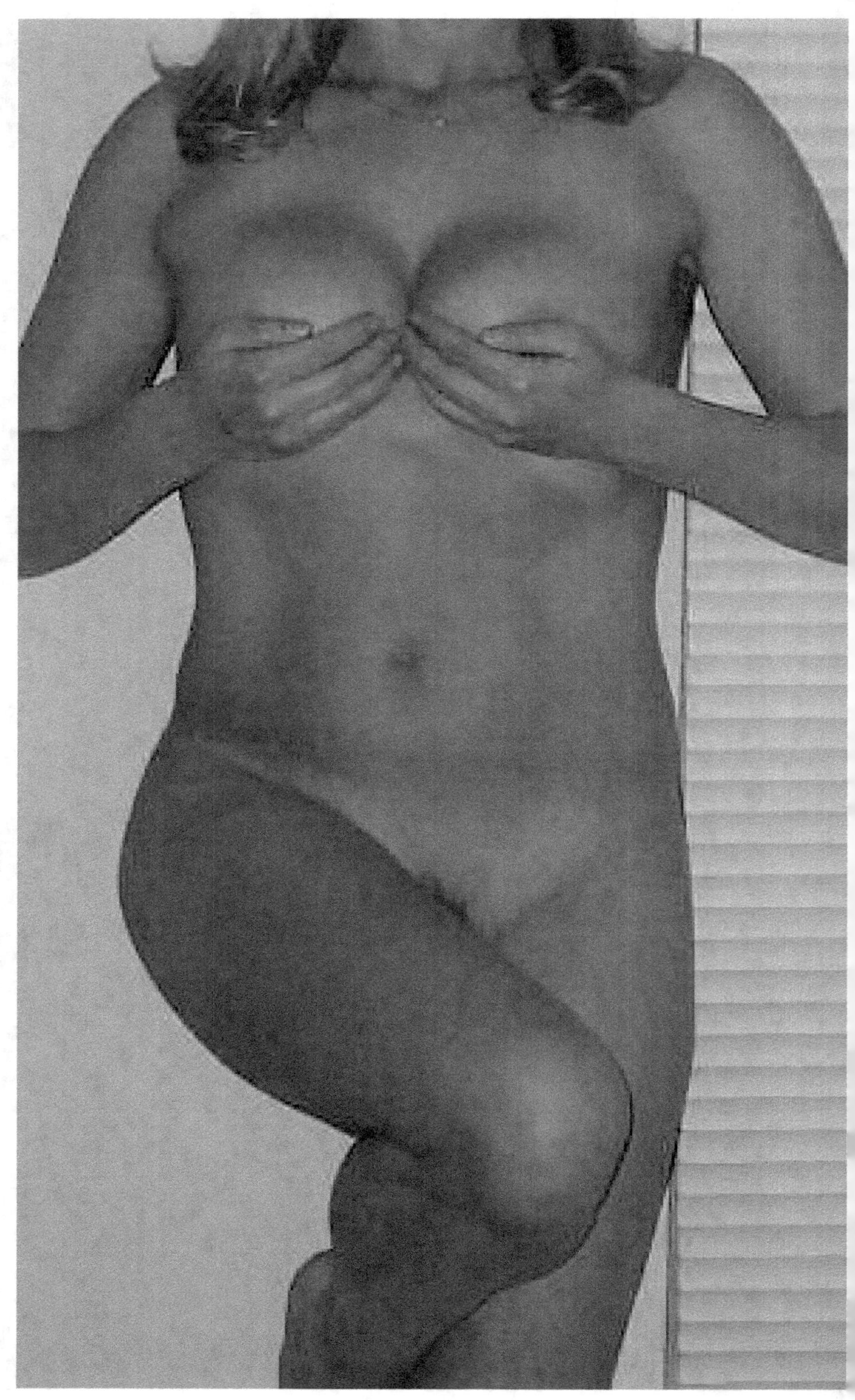

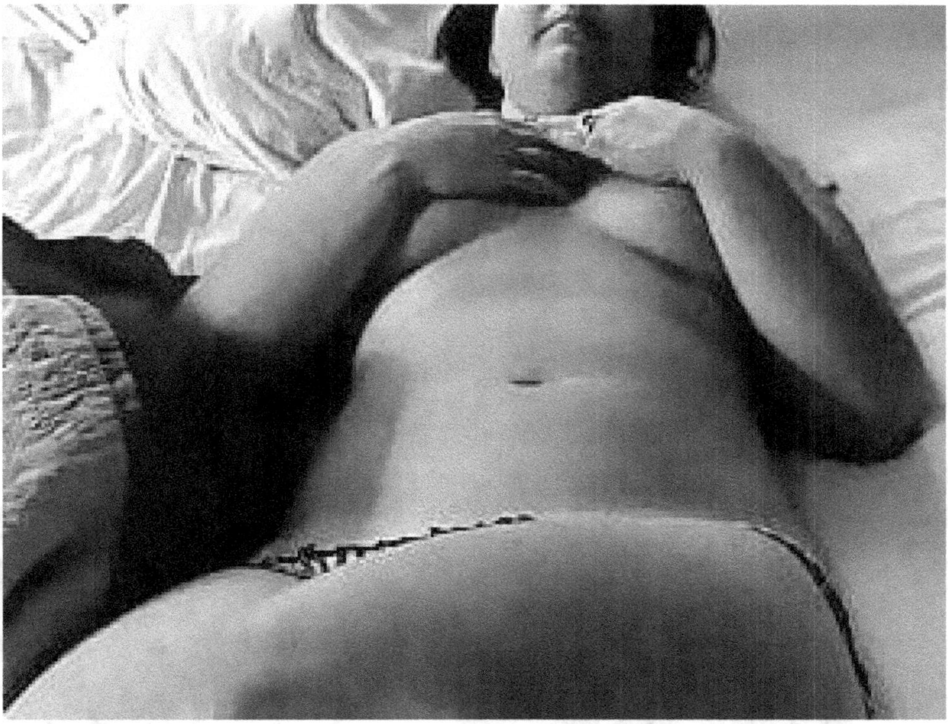

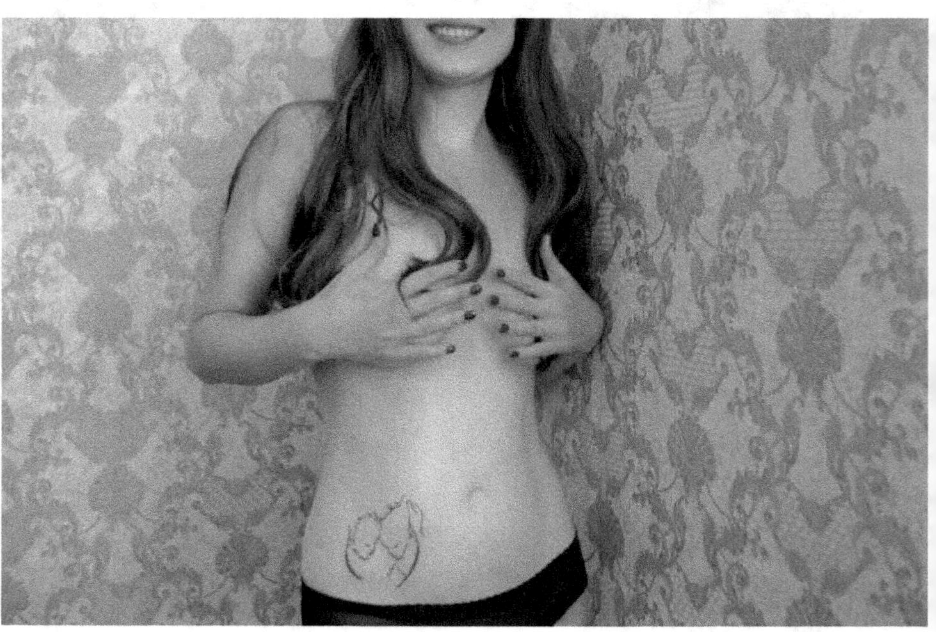

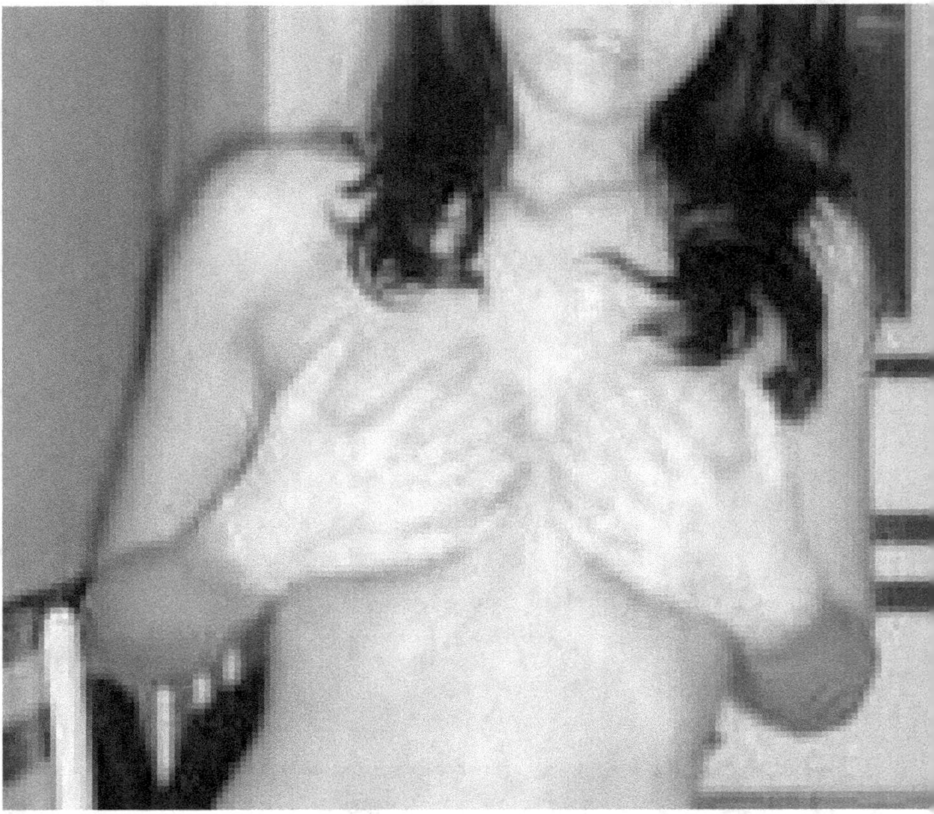

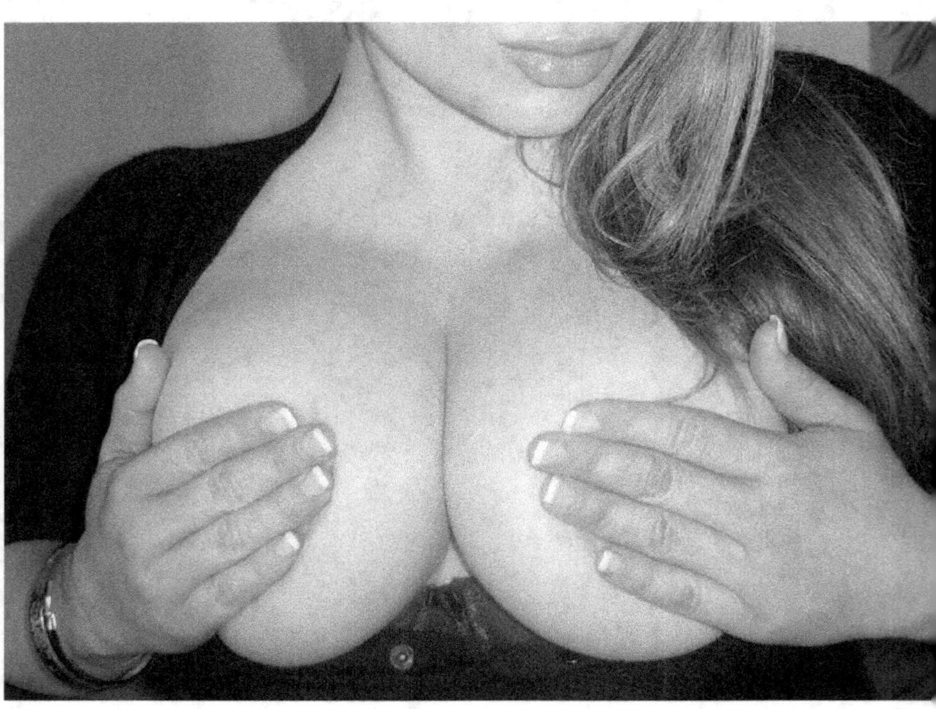

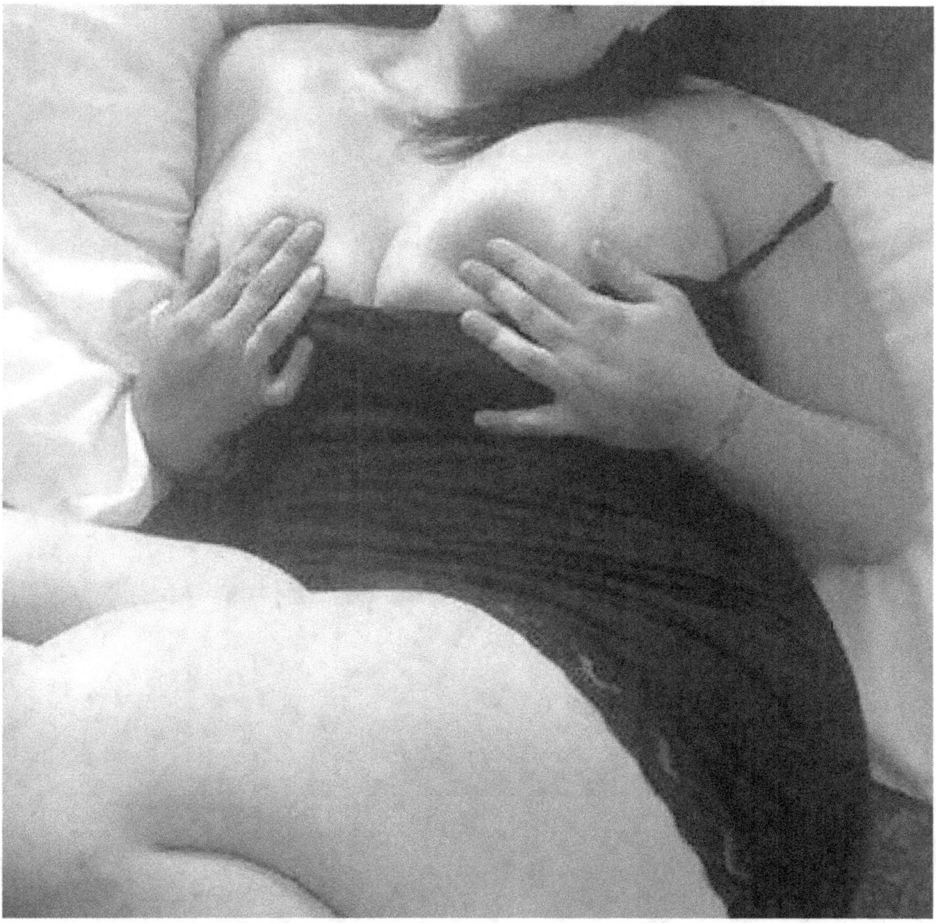

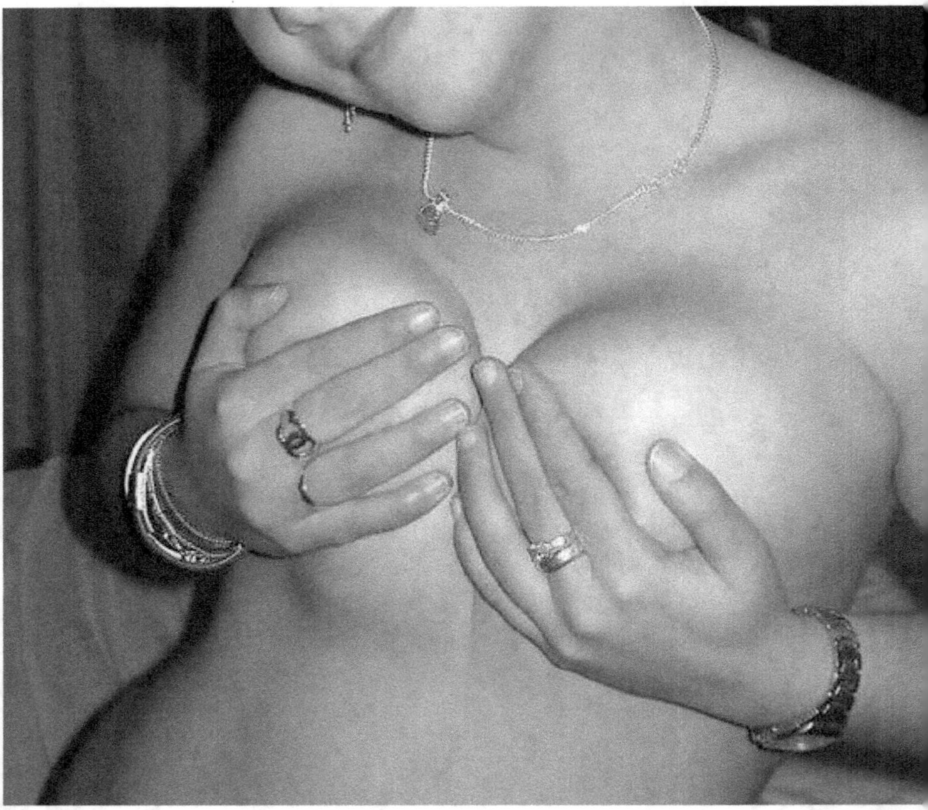

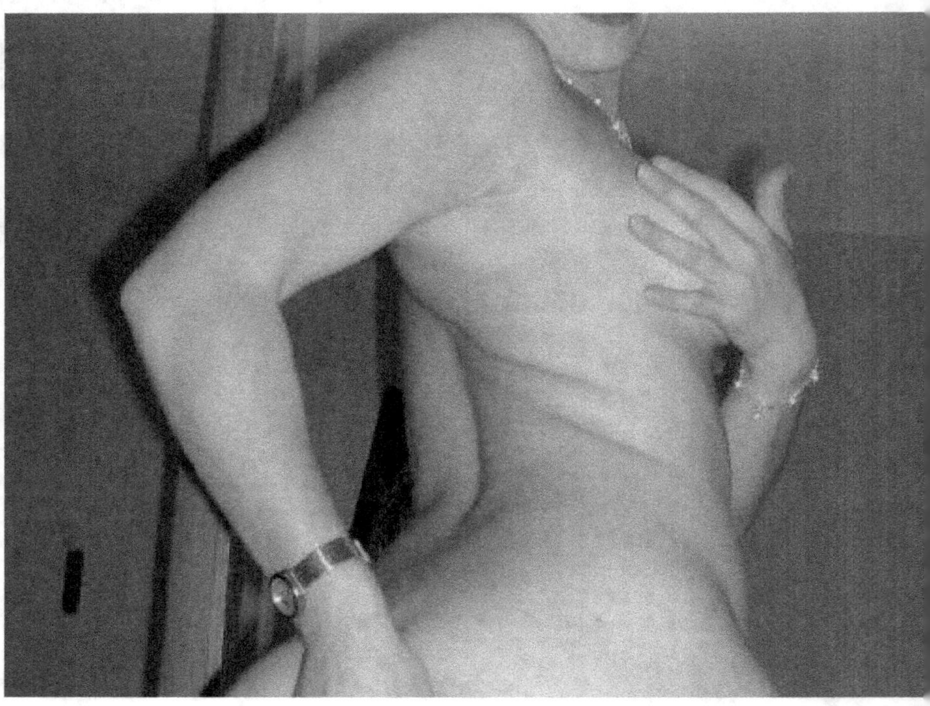

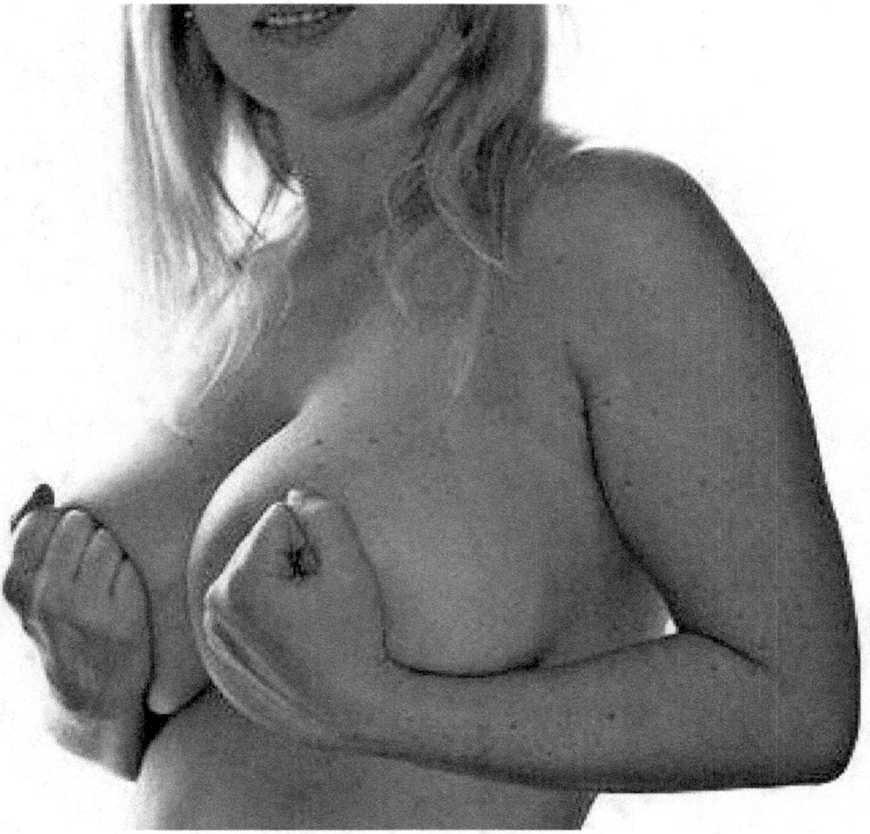

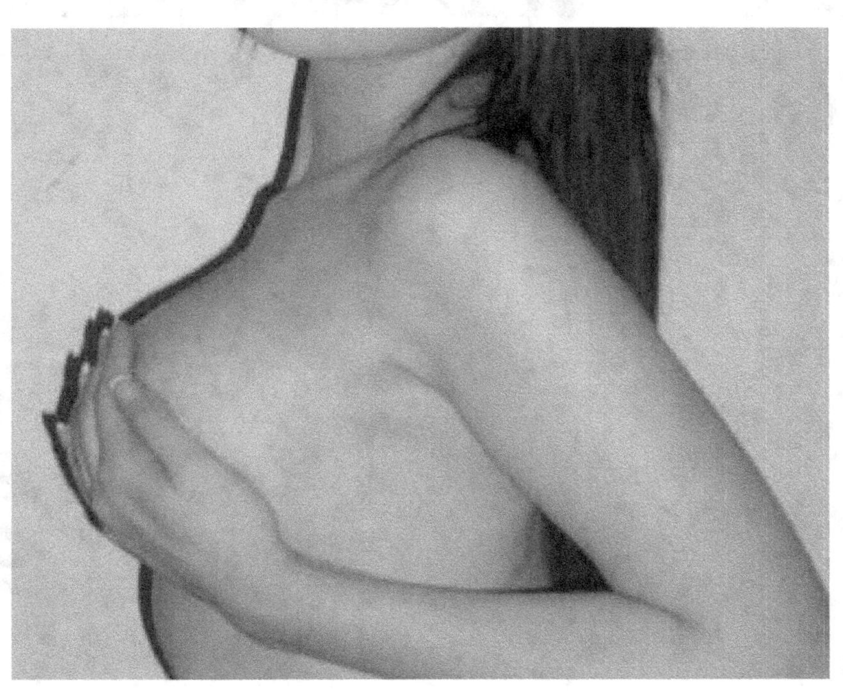

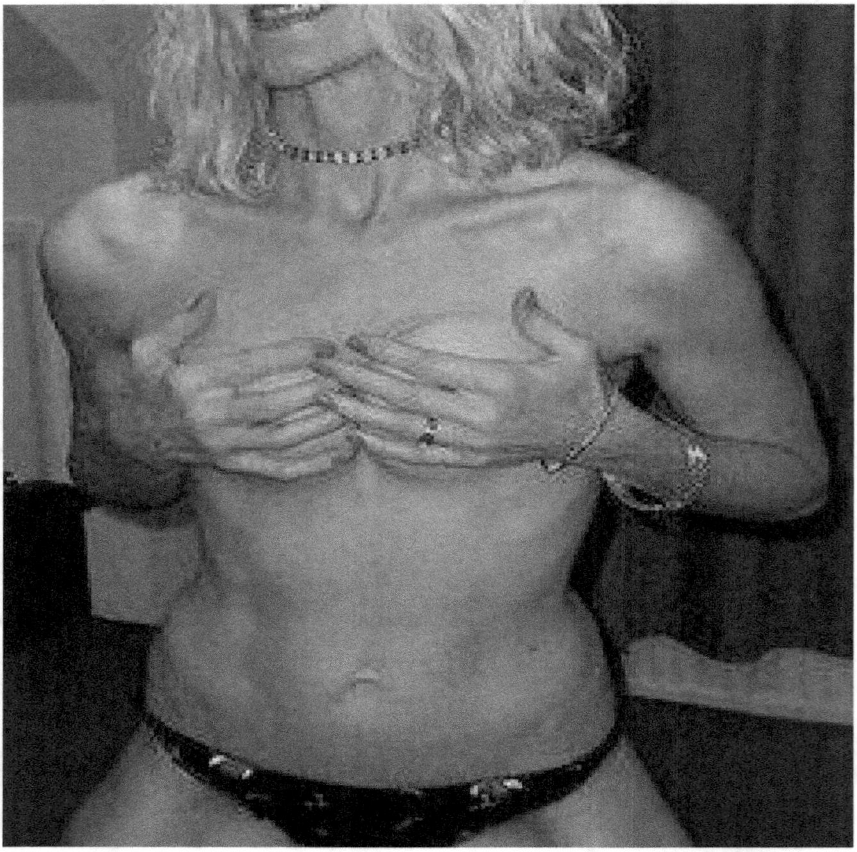

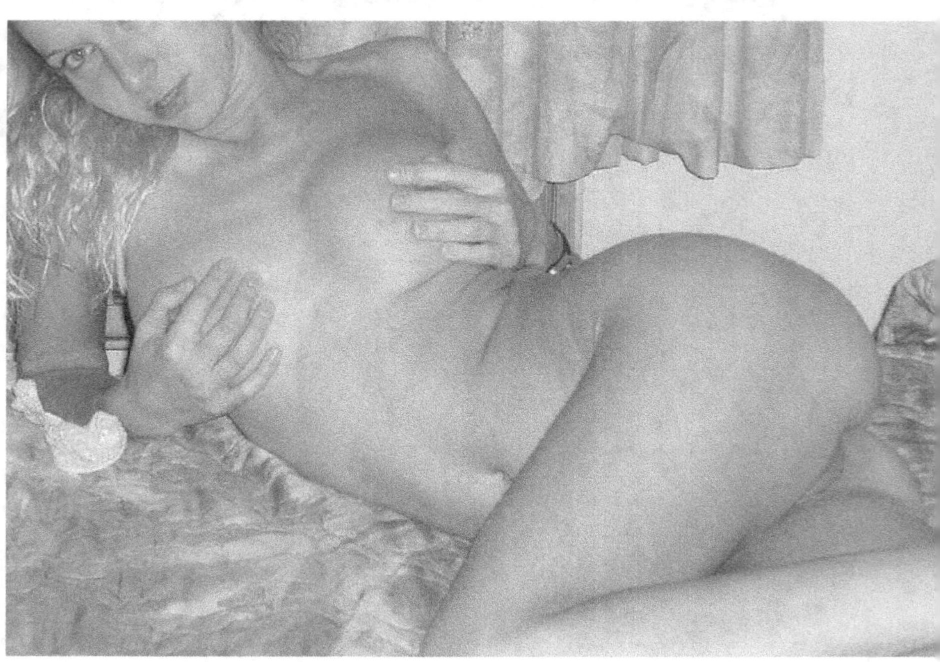

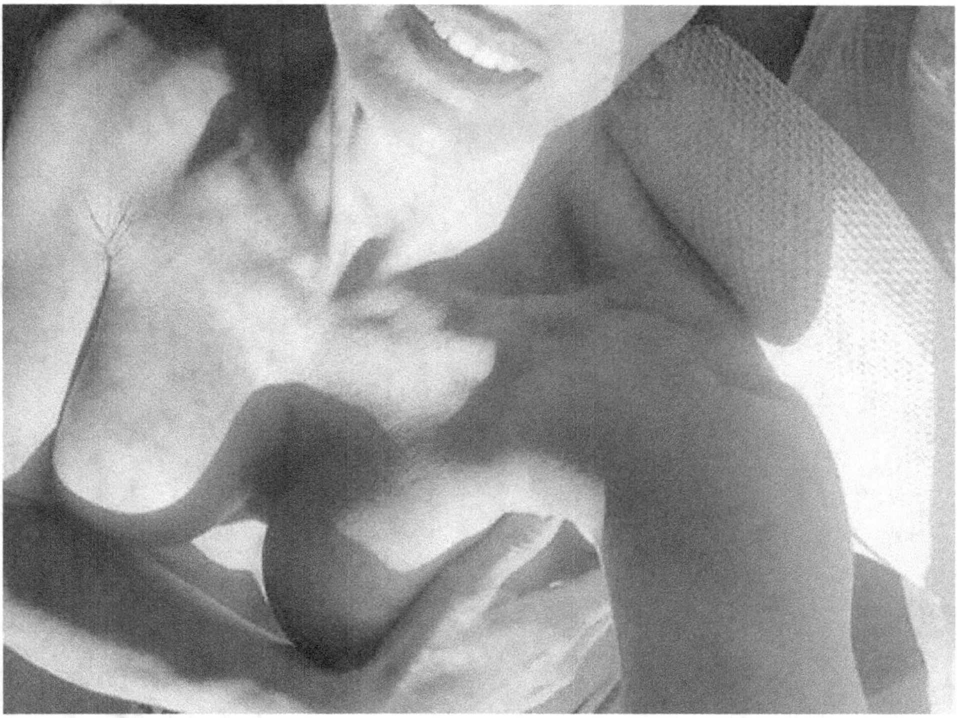

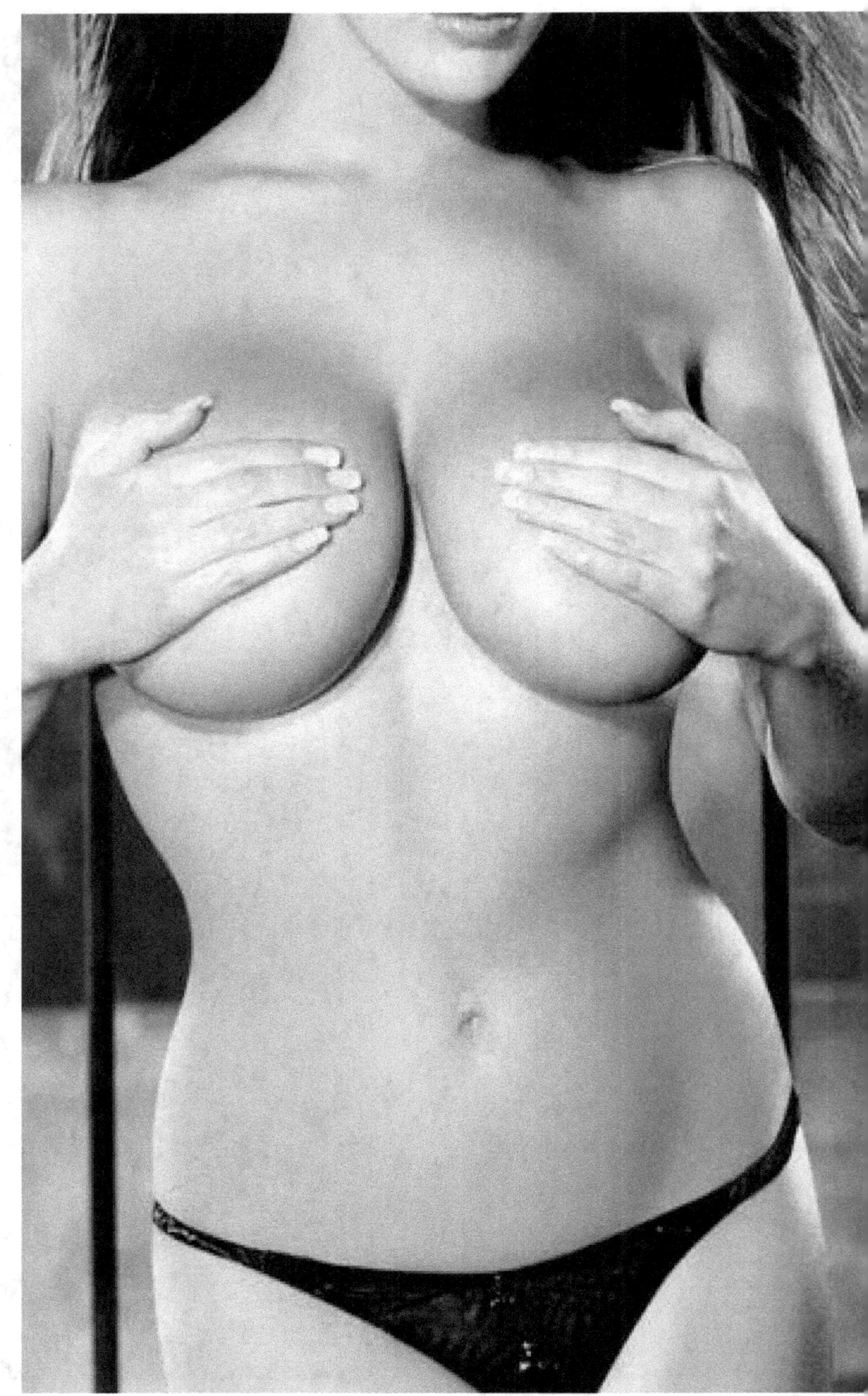

The many pictures displayed above narrate a story that even after voluntarily taking off the brassieres from their bodies, these girls perhaps by instinct, cover their plump big boobs with their arms preventing others from seeing their nude breasts.

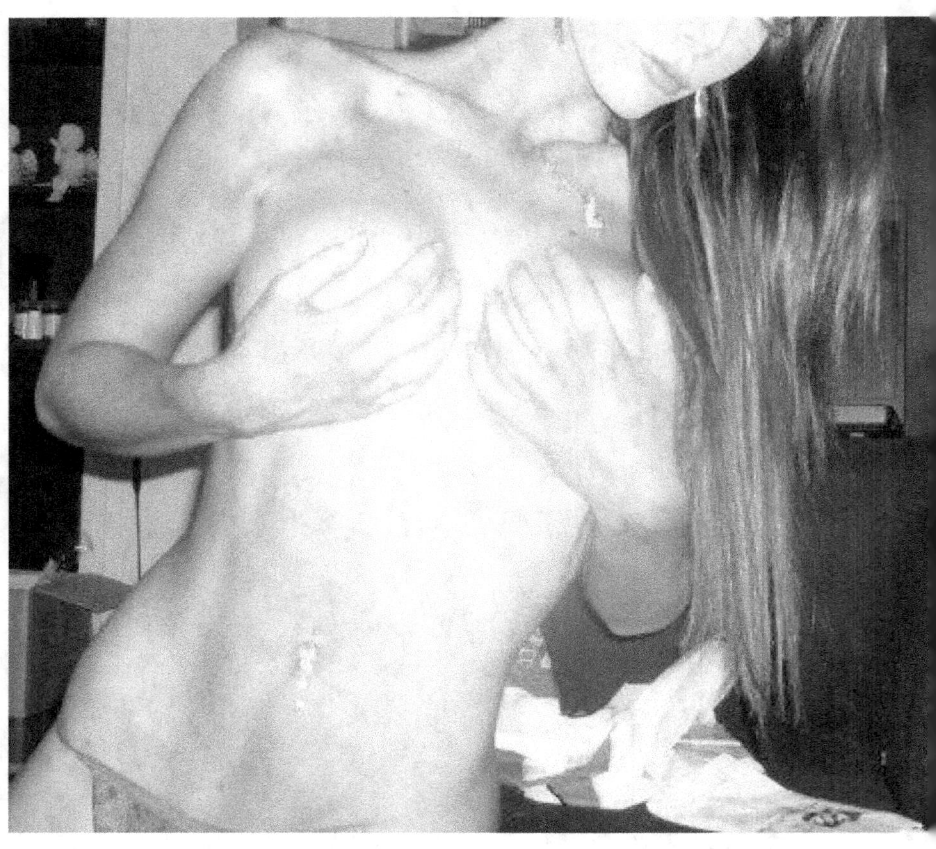

It looks like what has been mentioned on the afore-mentioned page seems to be true with this girl too. She too after removing her blouse and bra on her own accord or perhaps at the request of somebody, for the purpose of taking a photo, turns bashful and covers her naked pair of breasts with both her palms.

The picture reproduced below portrays the manner in which a girl has gone totally nude and in order to conceal her intimate parts, i.e. her vagina and breasts, covers them with her two hands, the right hand covering her breasts and her left hand her clean-shaven/hair-removed (depilated) vagina. She being a right-hander, by making use of her right hand to cover her breasts, does it subliminally and mysteriously connote that she attributes more importance and significance to her breasts than to her vagina where visibility and exposure are concerned?

# 02. Some Manifestations of the Concept of Boobieshandsstraps

## 2.1. The Female doing the boobieshandsstrap on her own accord/on her own free will instinctively

This manifestation is the most common form of boobieshandsstraps which women do instinctively, perhaps caught unawares whilst they remain topless or fully naked in

many situations, predominantly where the male population
is present. The following pictures illustrate this situation:

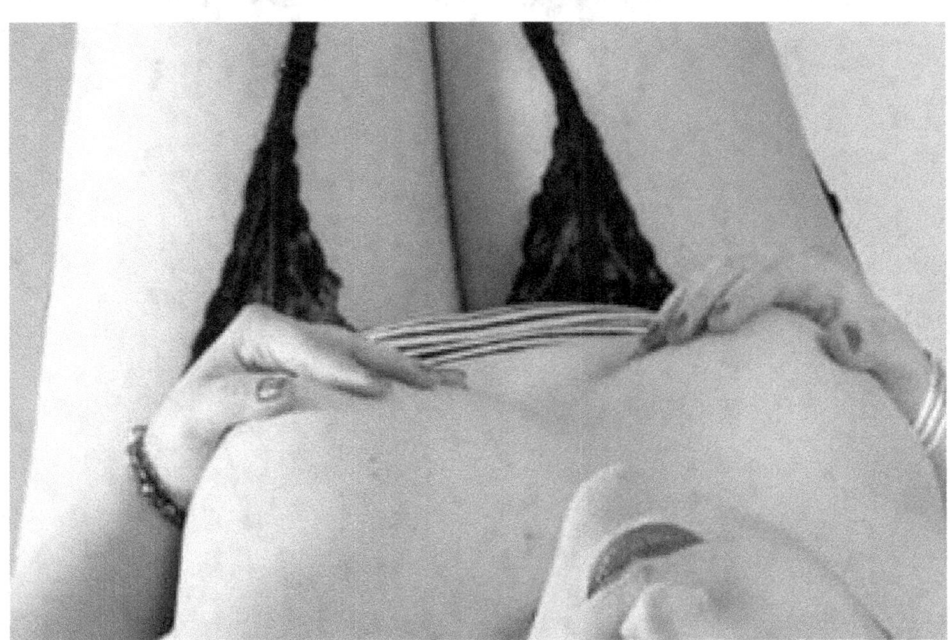

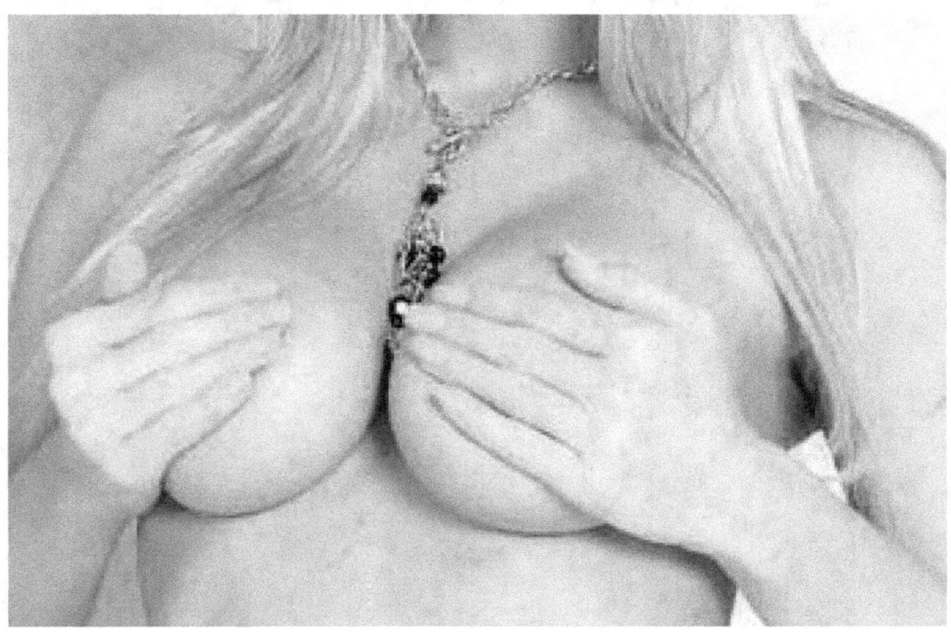

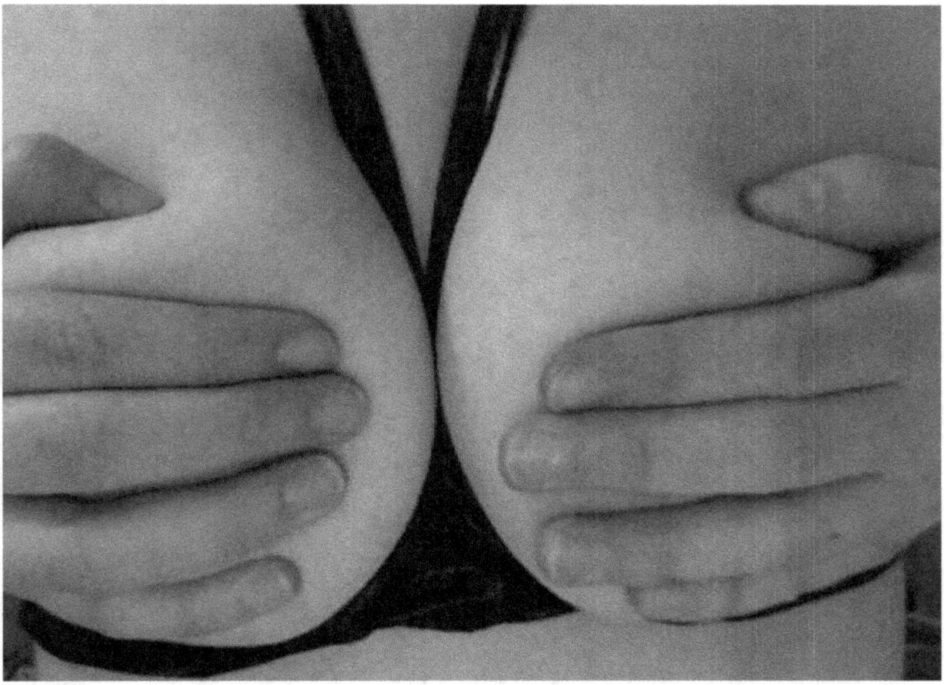

(This occurs in a self-orgasmic excitement situation wherein the girl instinctively boobieshandsstraps herself avoiding exposure)

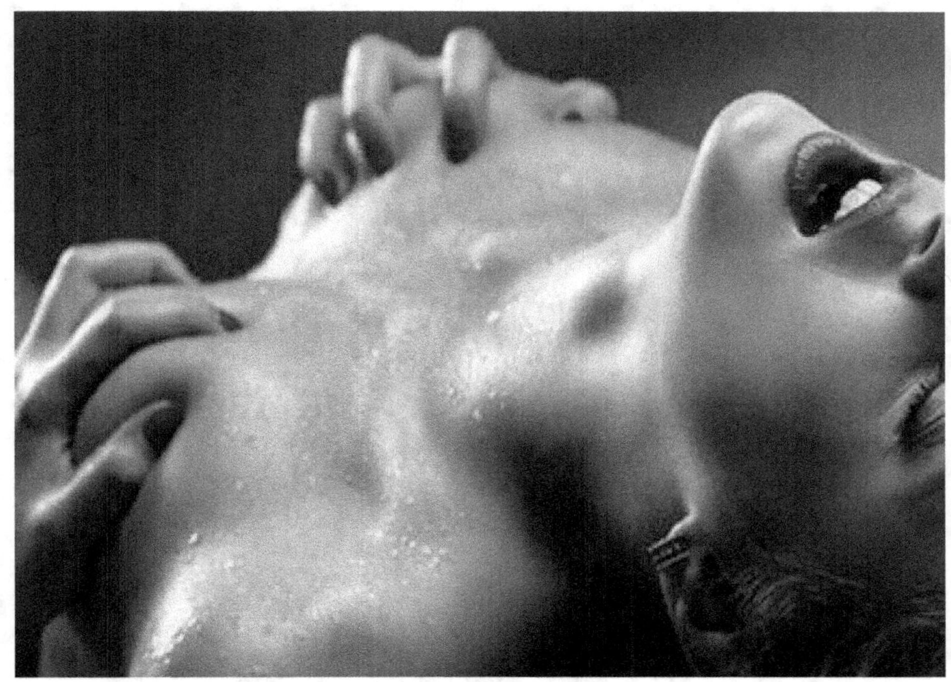

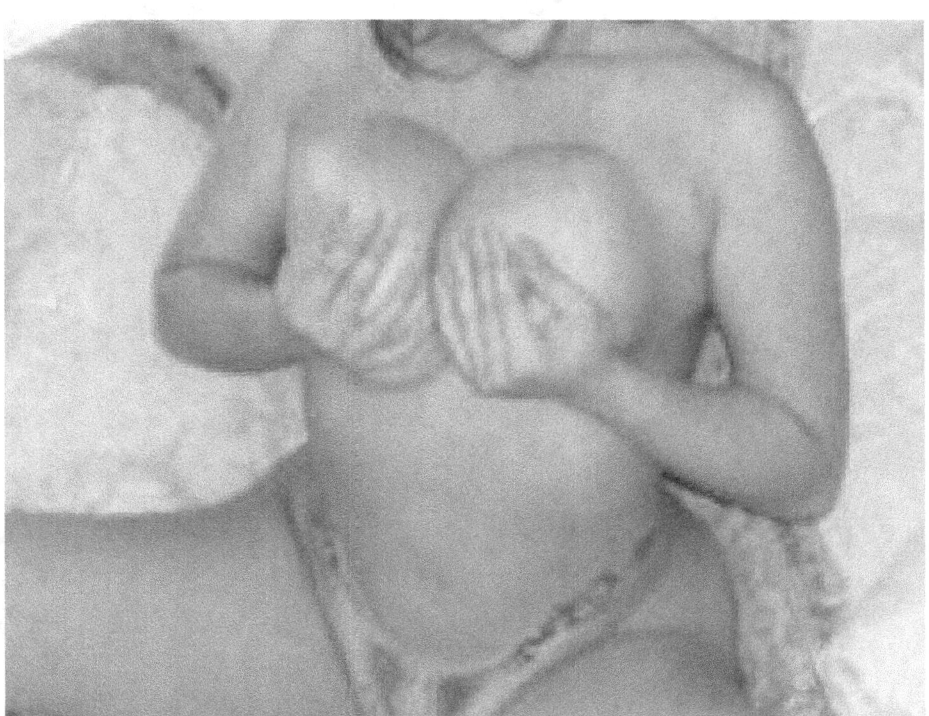

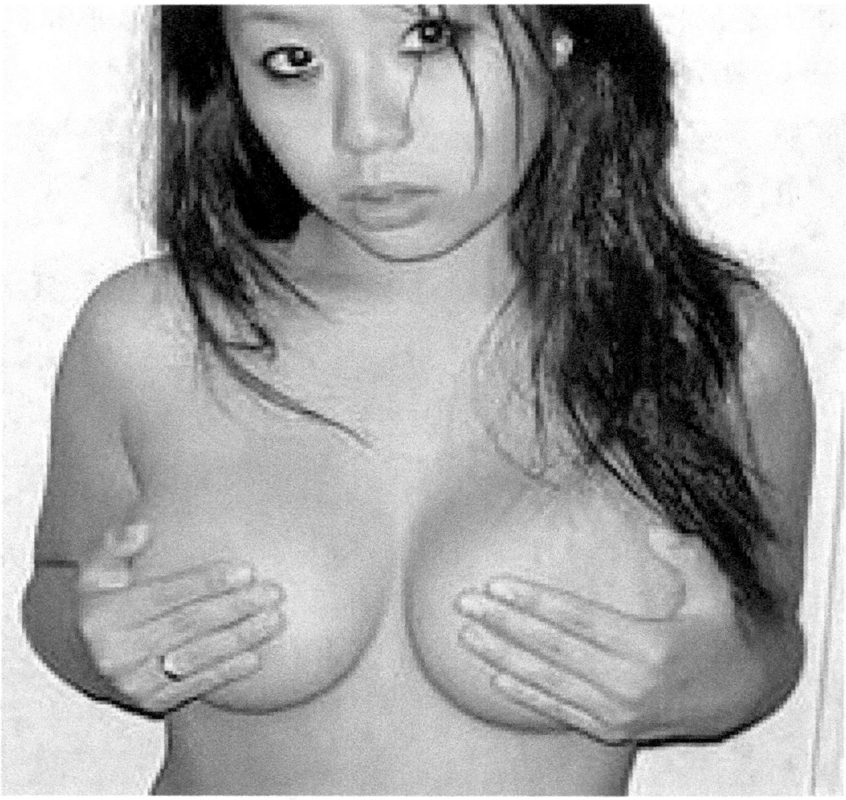

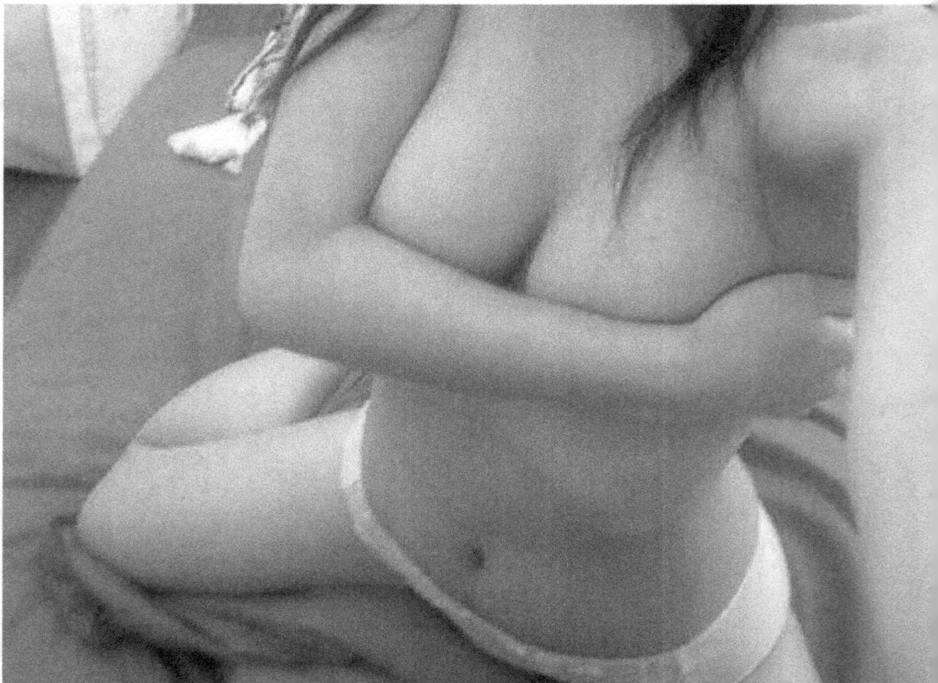

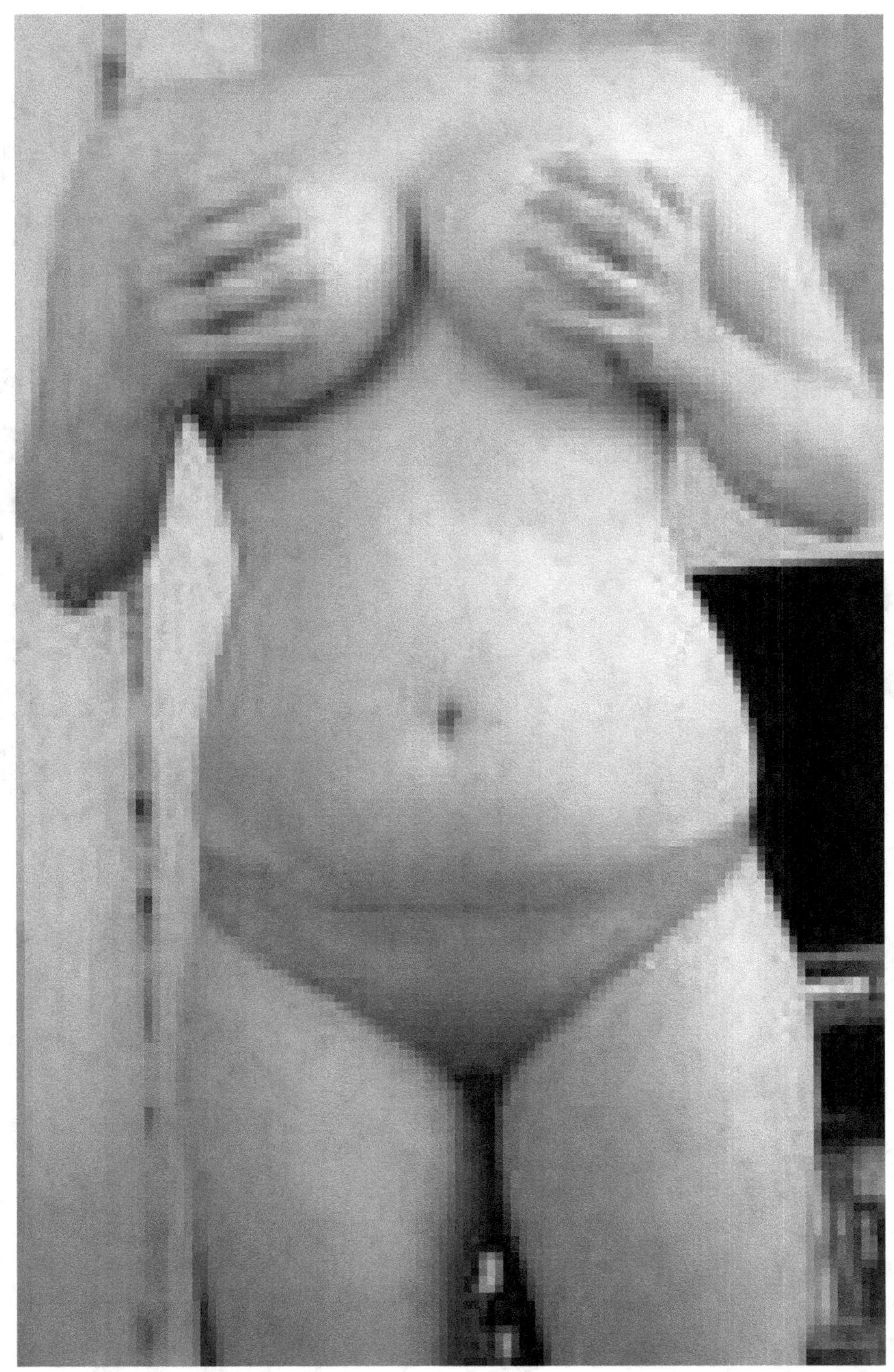

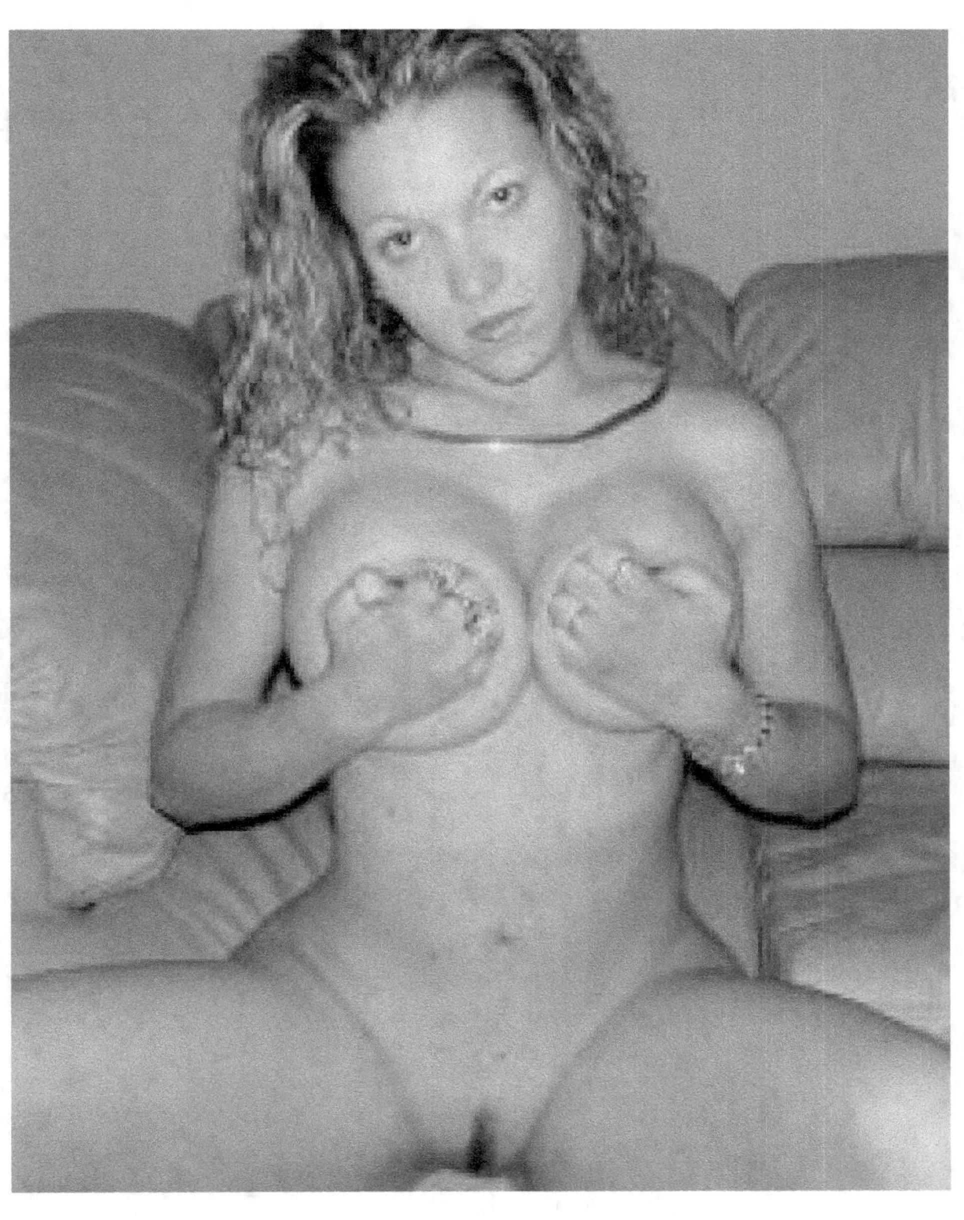

## 2.2. The female is assisted or supported by her male-lover/ boy-friend/husband to boobieshandsstrap by herself or by him wilfully

This situation is not very common as the one demonstrated earlier. However, where carnal and erotic manifestations are concerned, this situation becomes the most sought after by both genders-male and female. The following pictures will amply exemplify this phenomenon:

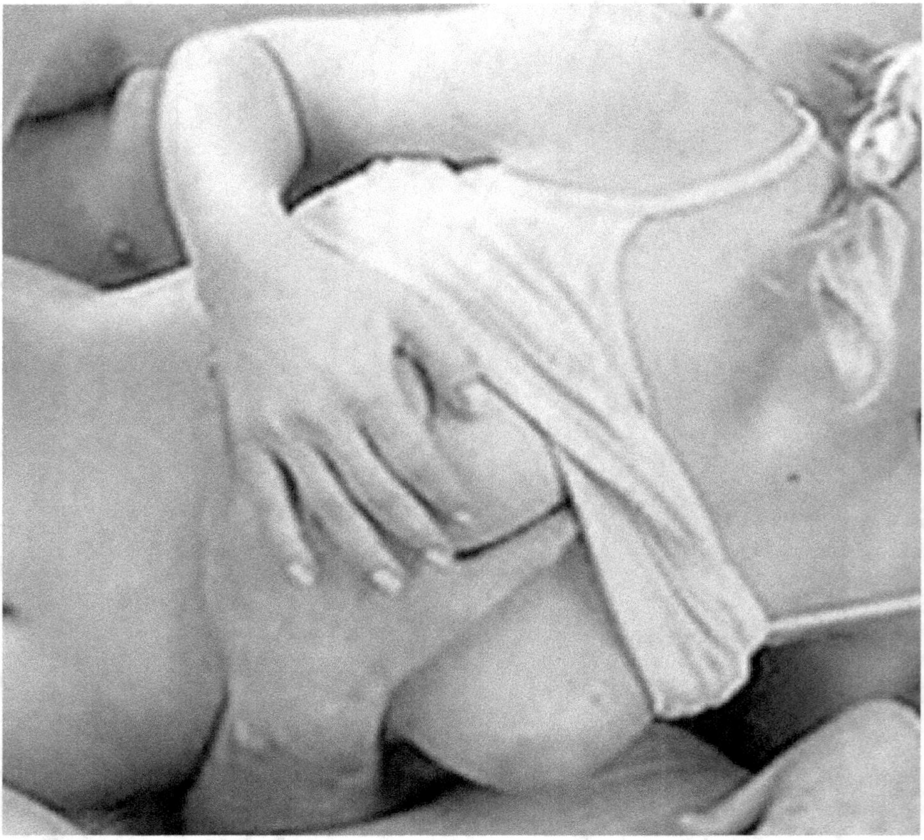

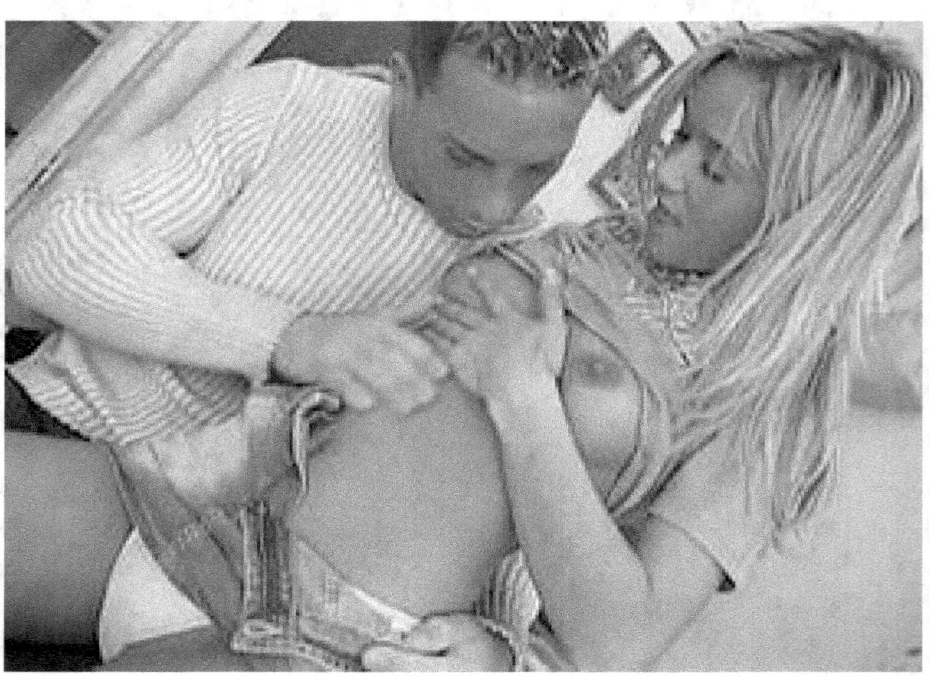

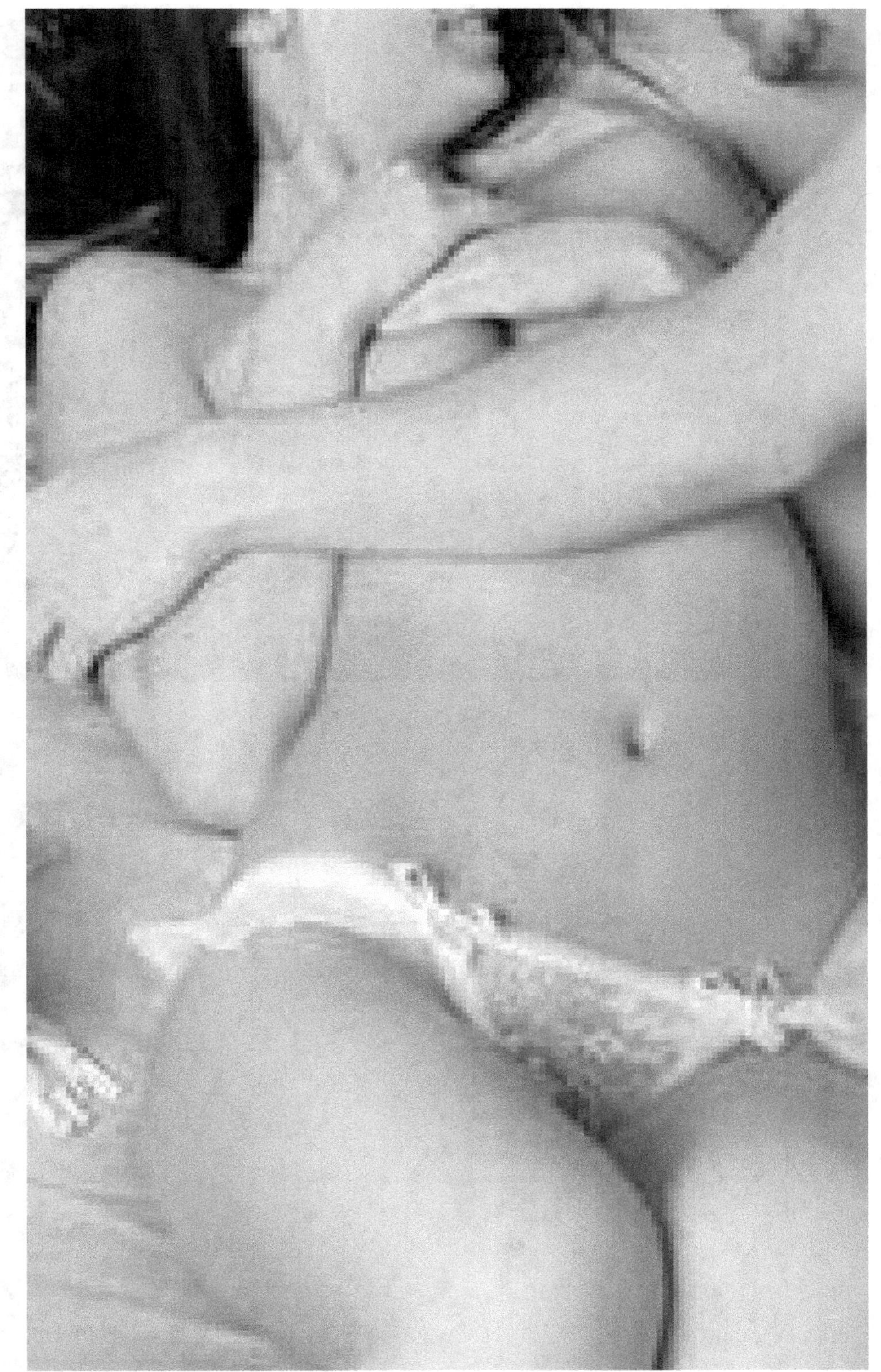

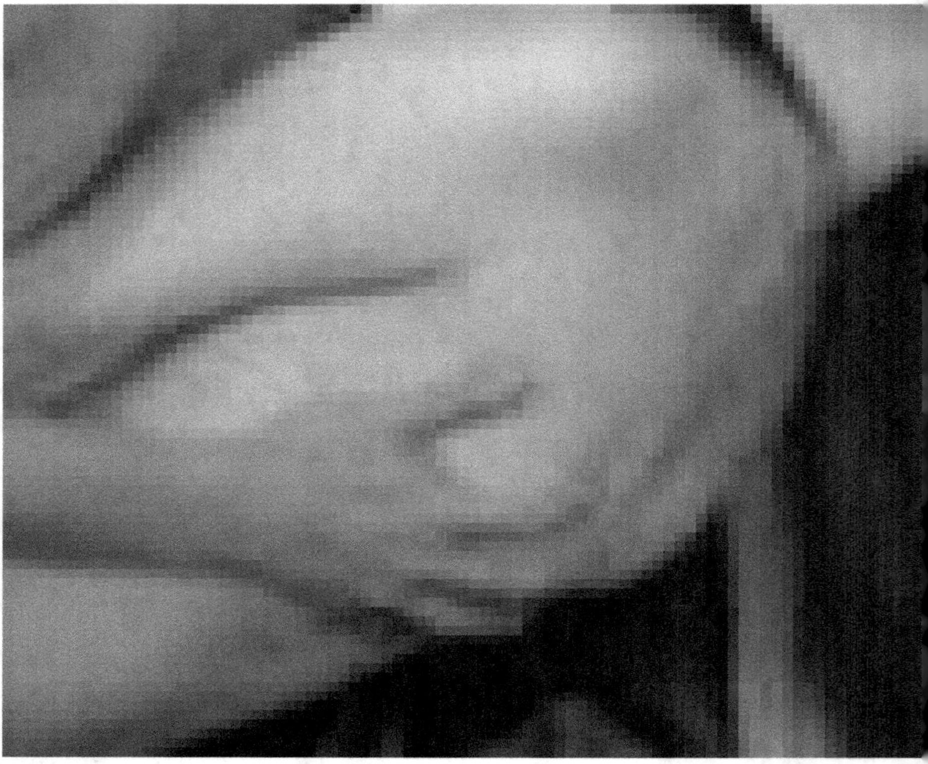

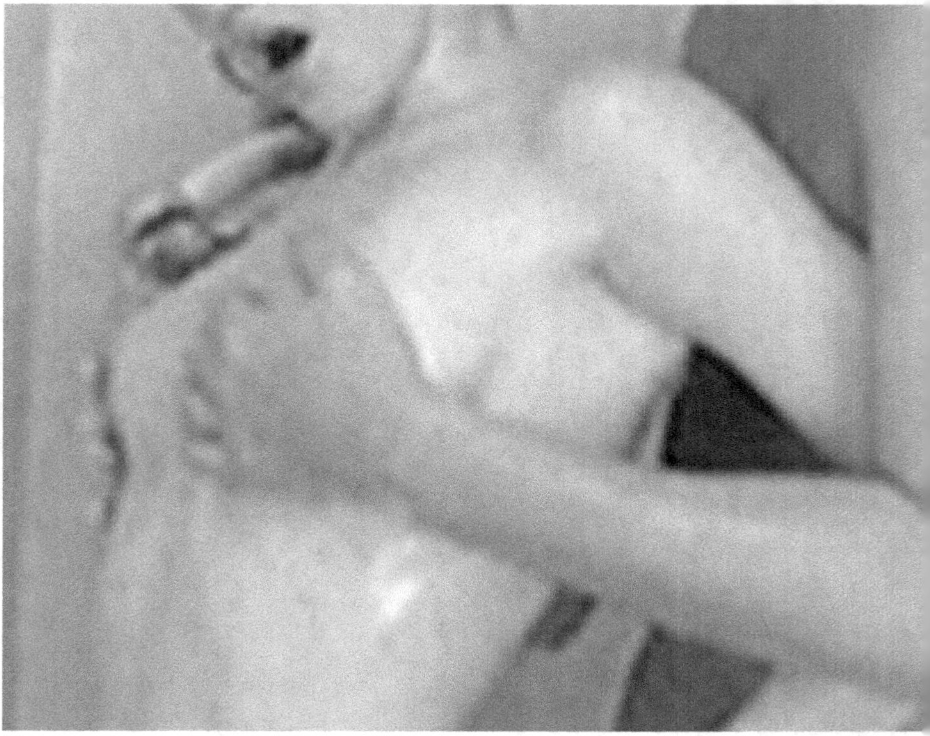

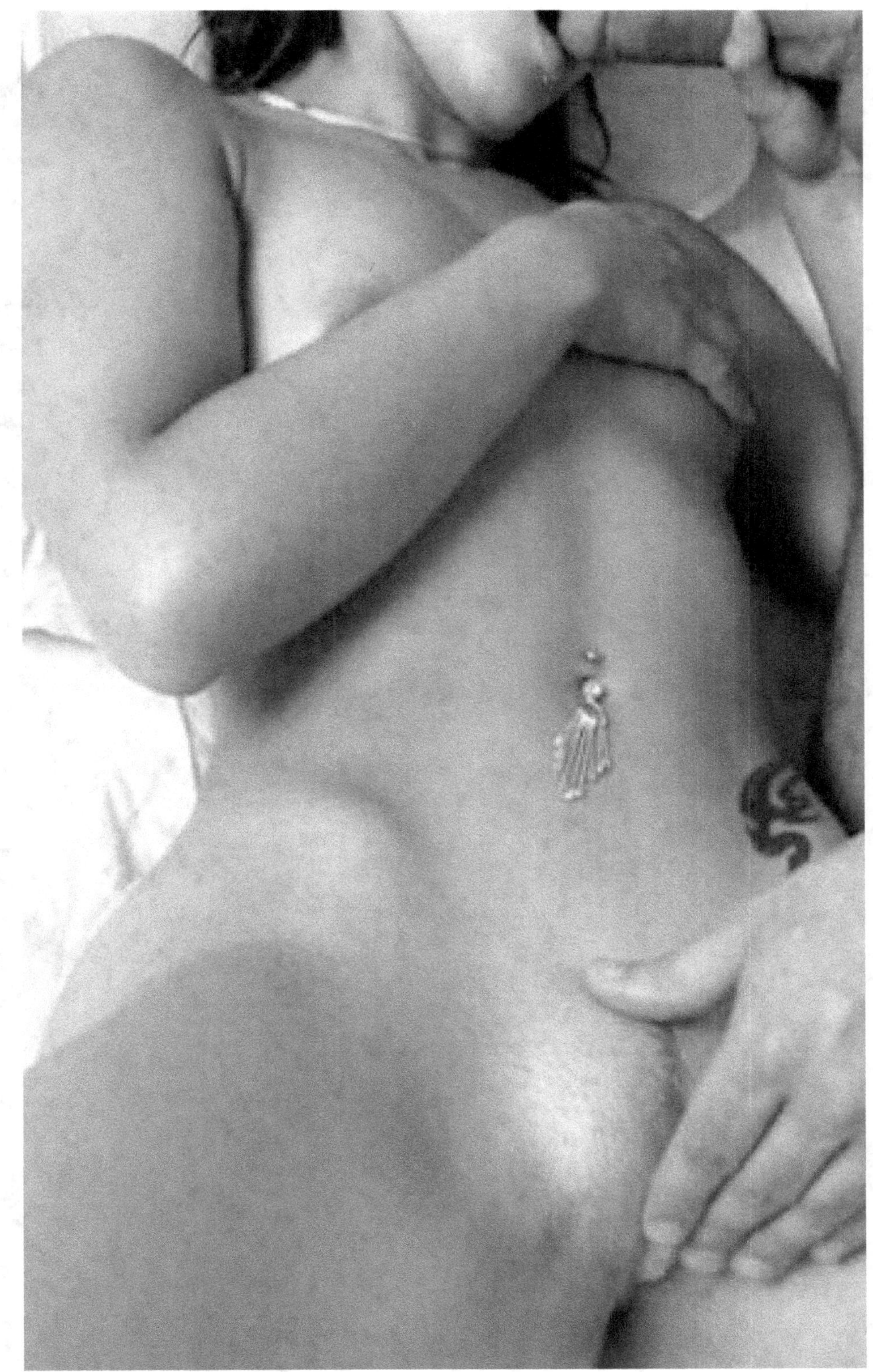

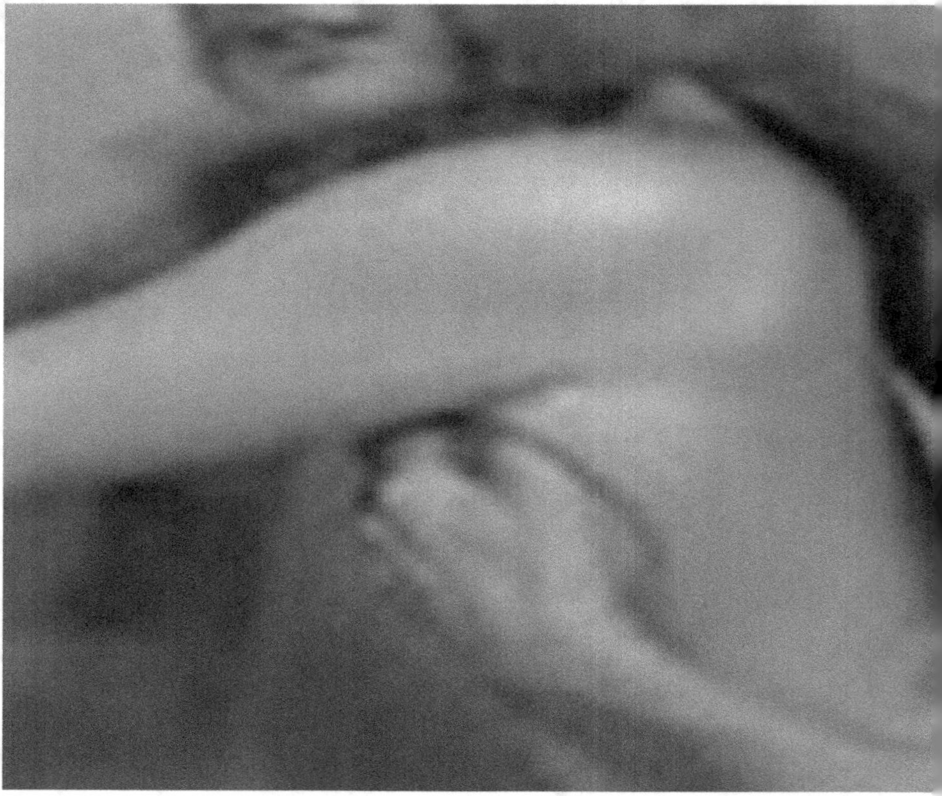

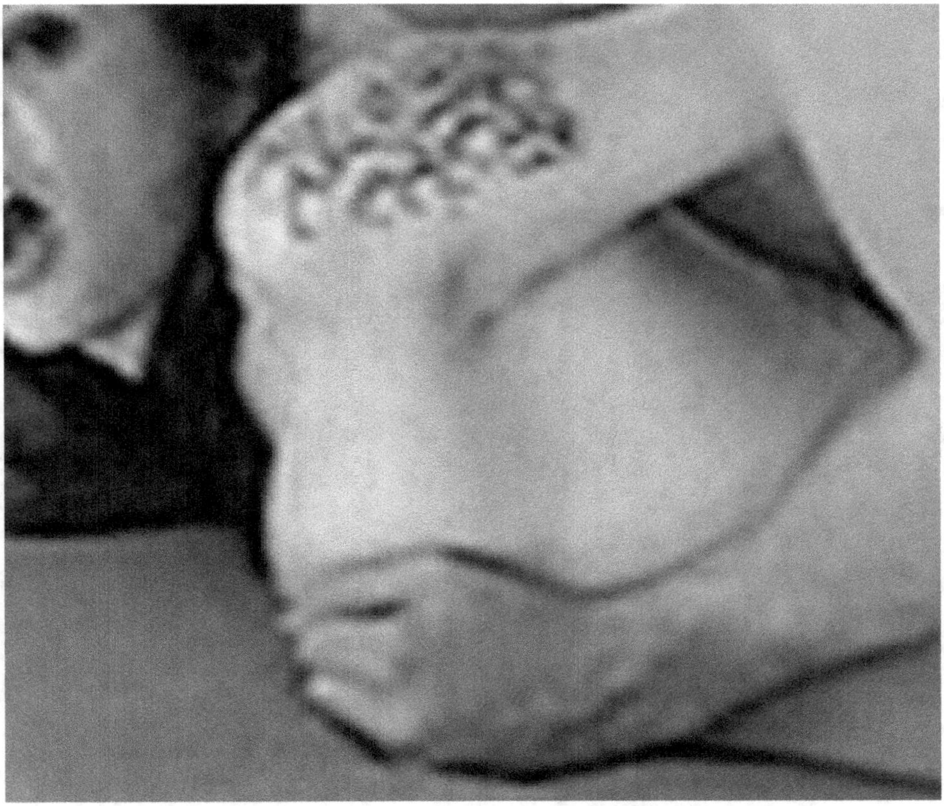

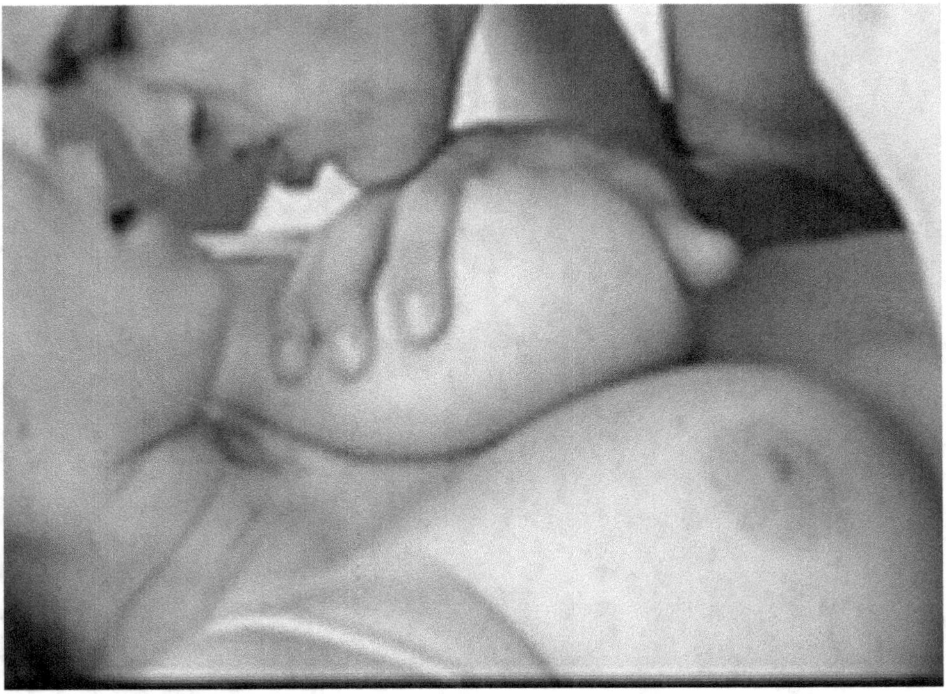

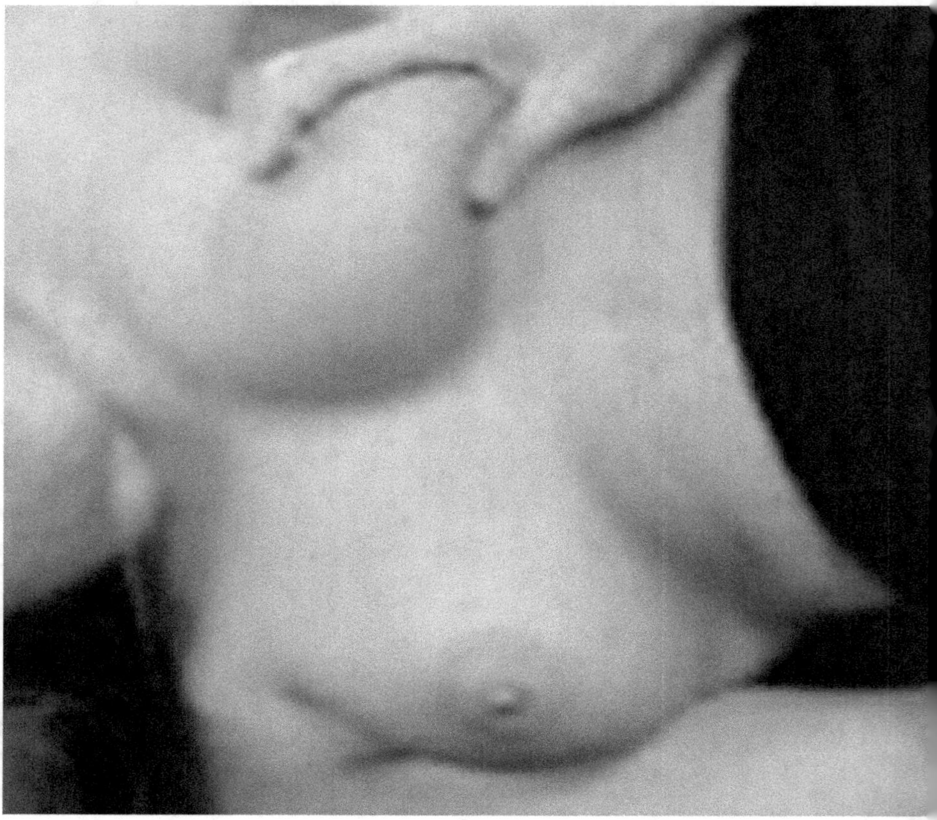

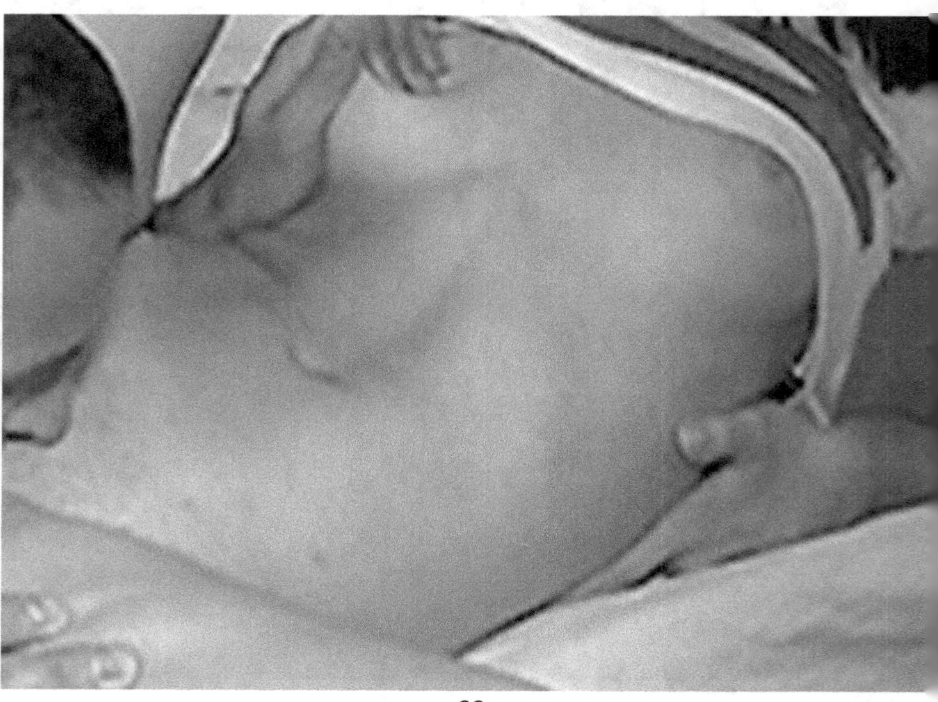

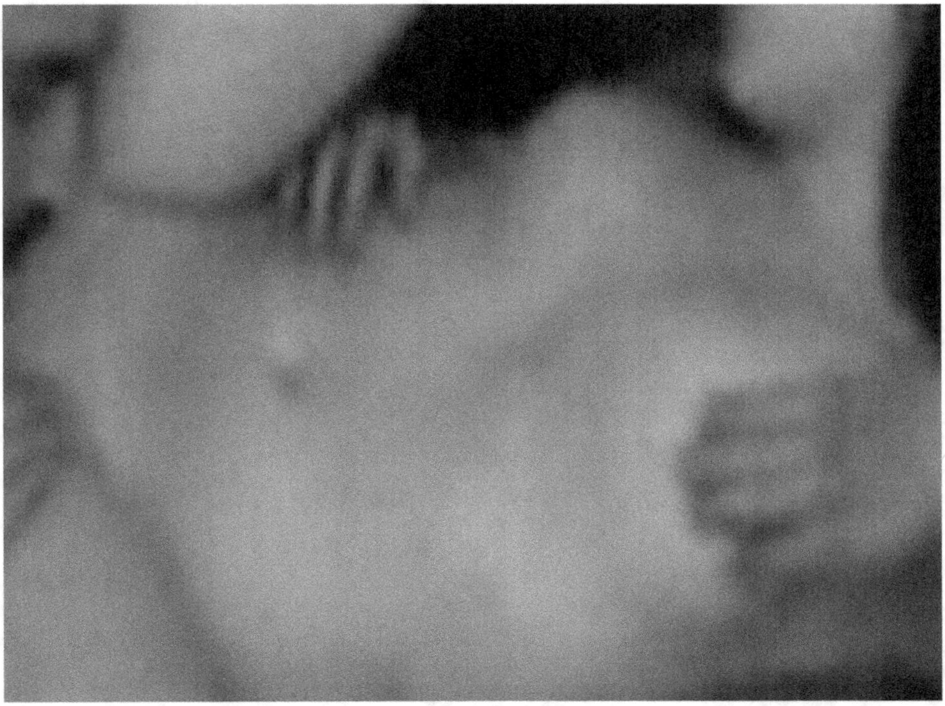

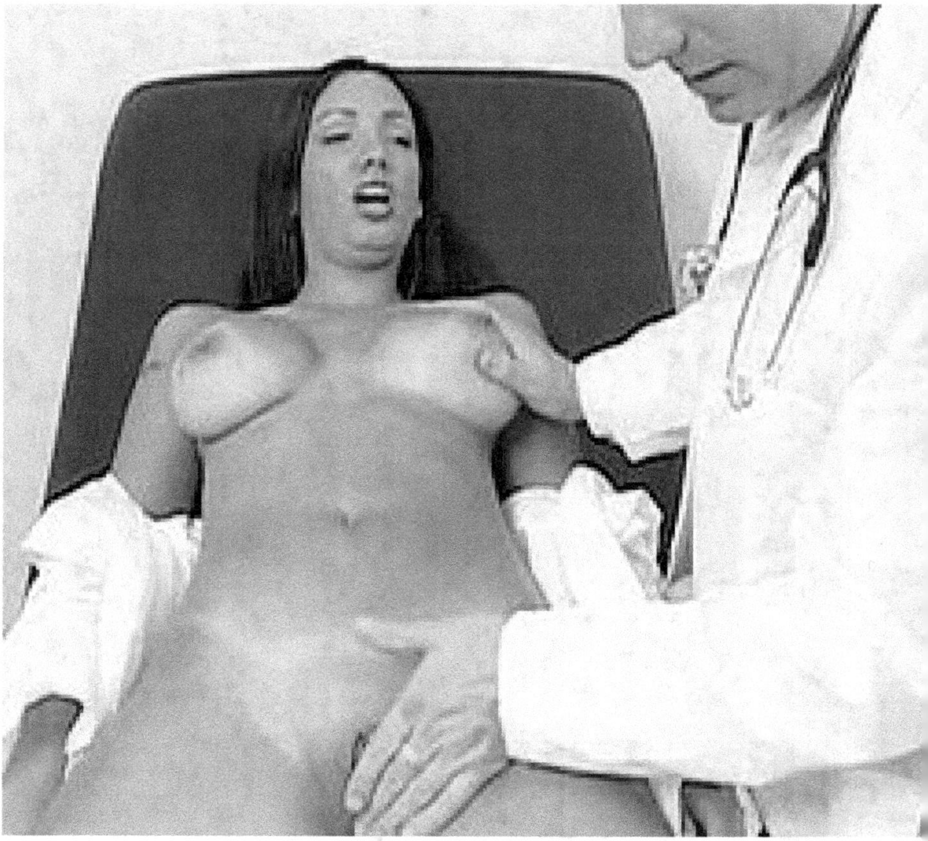

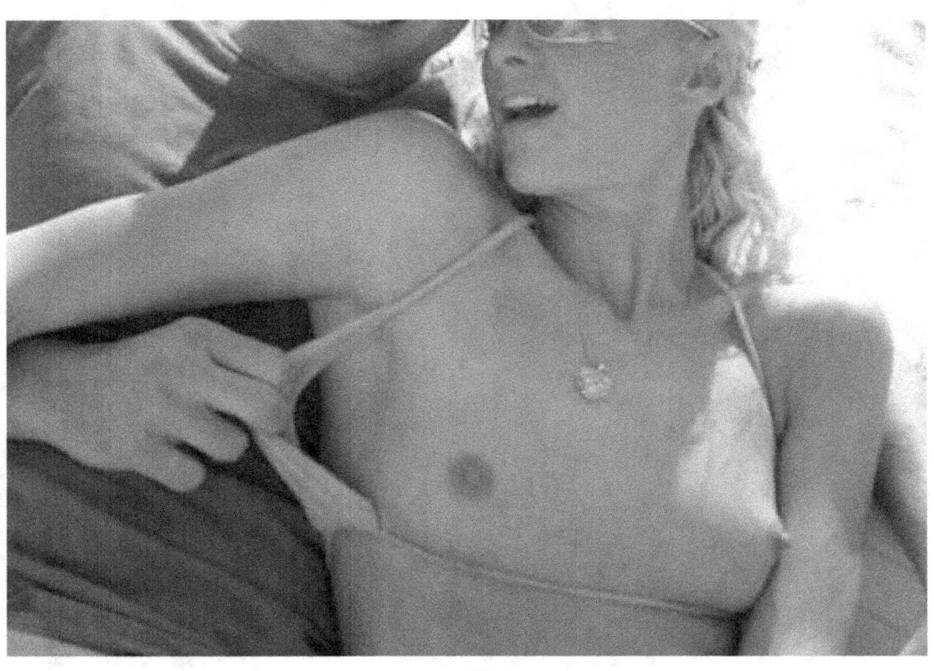

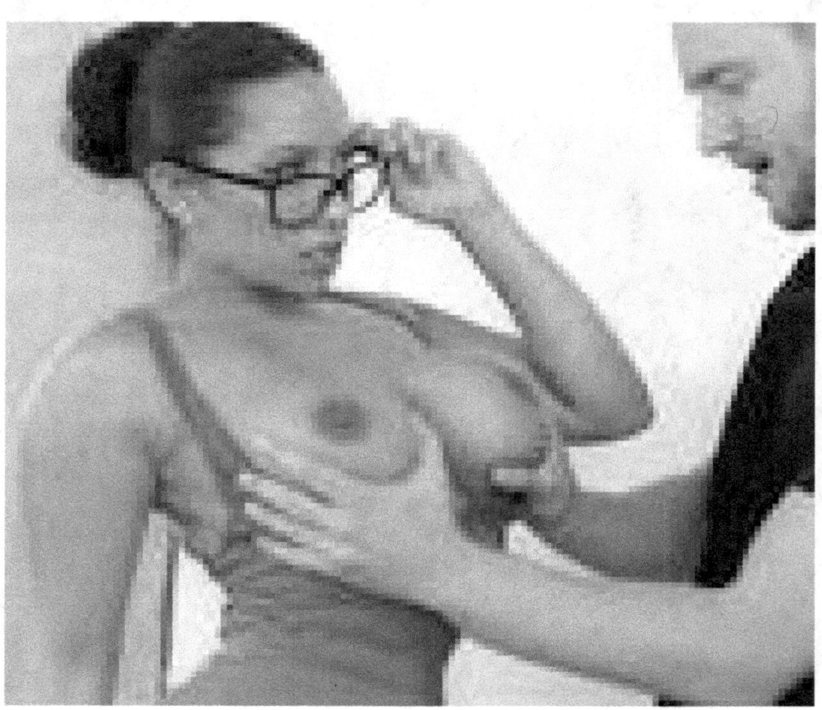

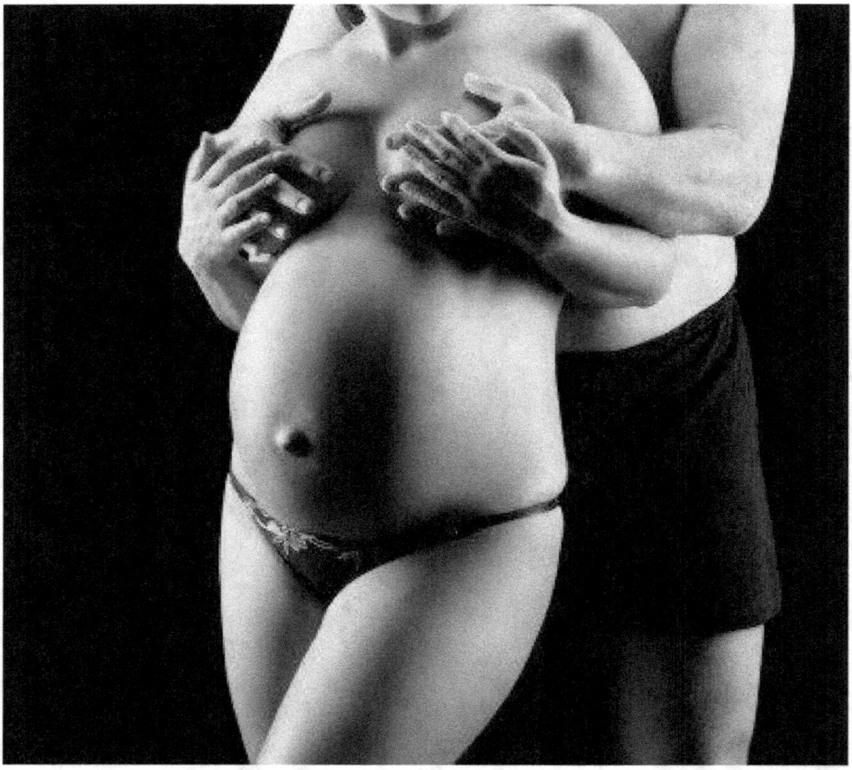

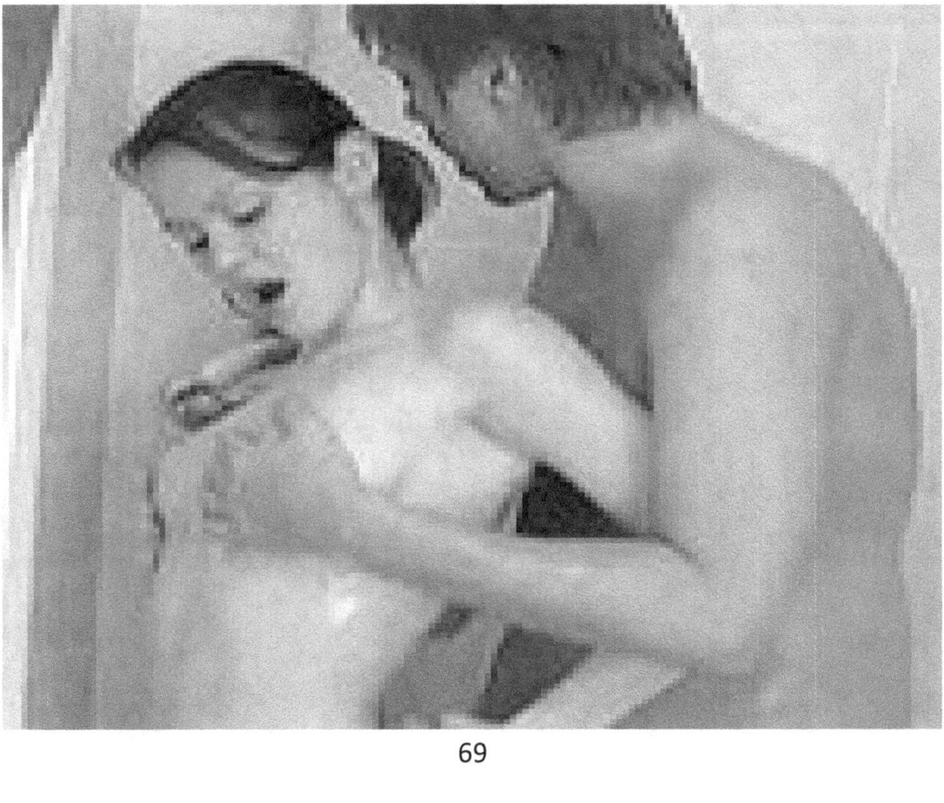

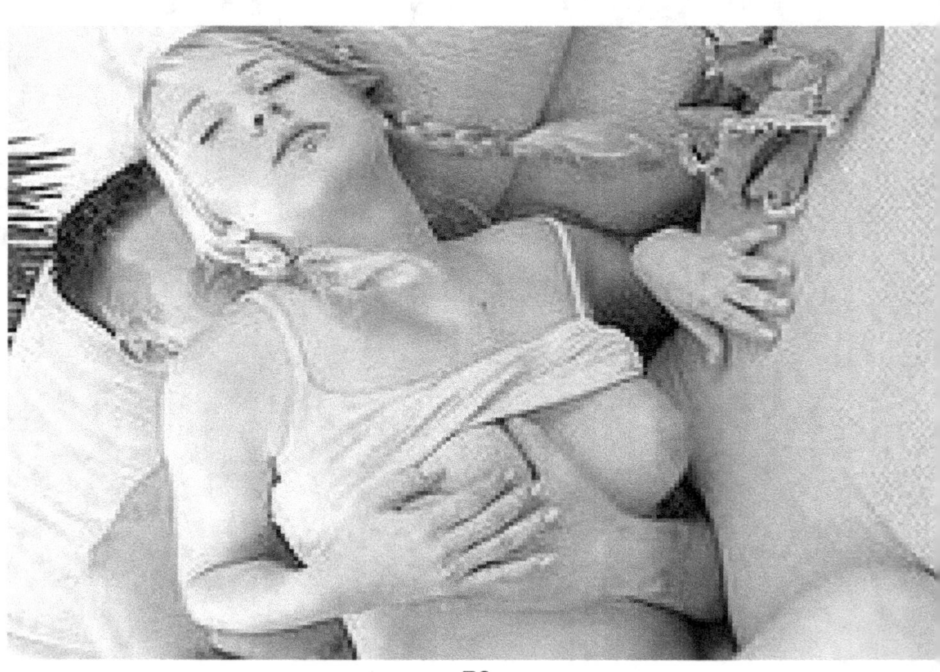

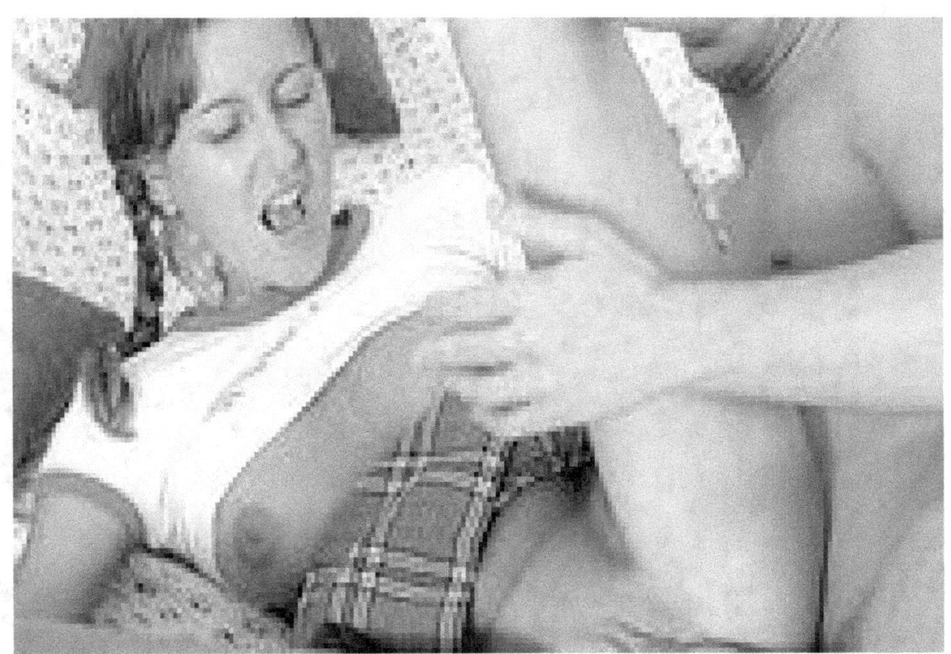

## 2.3. The Female is assisted or supported by her girl-friend/ friends to do the boobieshandsstraps wilfully

This trend or situation too seems to be quite common particularly among young girls and young women in a friendly atmosphere. Indulging in such a practice does not necessarily connote that they possess lesbian tendencies and/or are professed lesbians. It is observed that irrespective of the age, nationality or race of the participants, the womenfolk the world over take pleasure in engaging in this harmless and innocent practice/pastime without arousing scandals or social odium.

The following pictures very candidly illustrate this phenomenon. Additionally, the writer has discovered some very rare and hard to find pictures falling into this category which package is presented with pleasure as a complementary bonus to the reader and the viewer for the primary purpose of their carnal and erotic satisfaction, pleasure and delight irrespective of their gender.

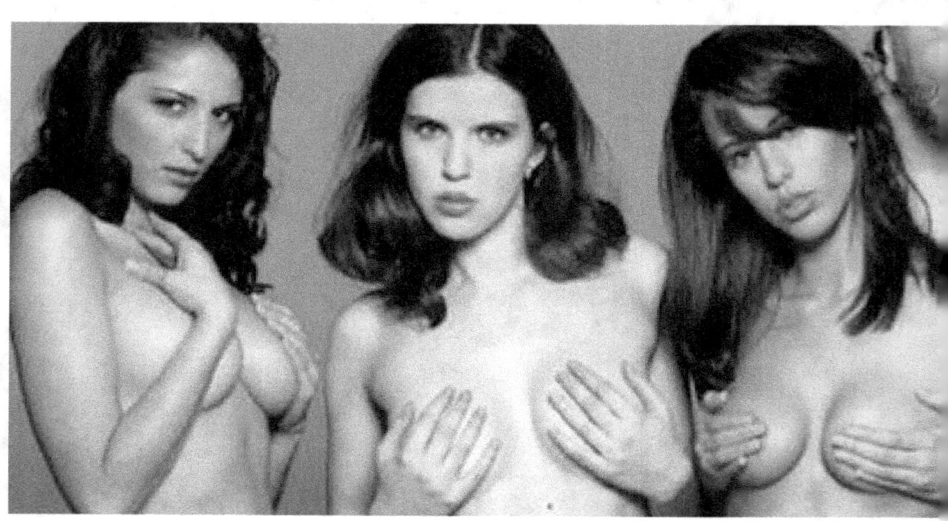

KAMASUTRA
SULEWSKA

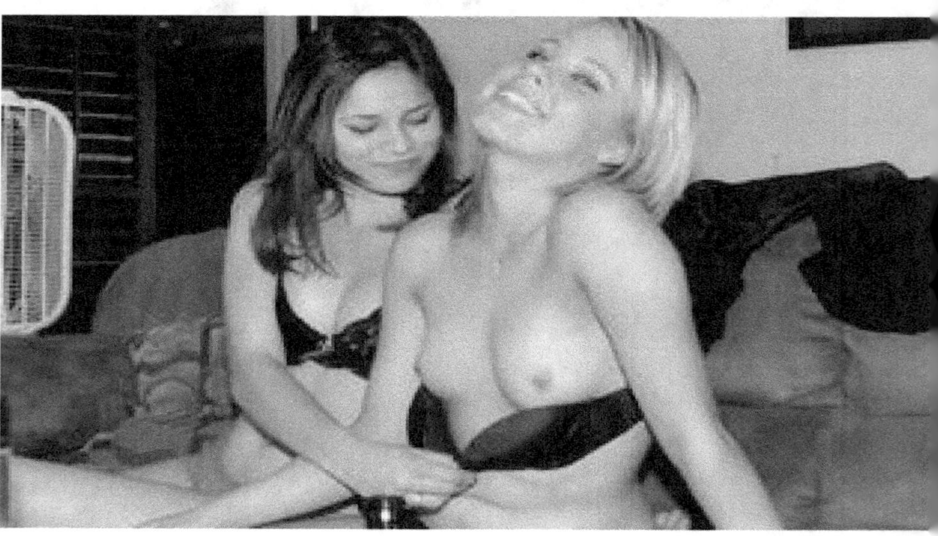

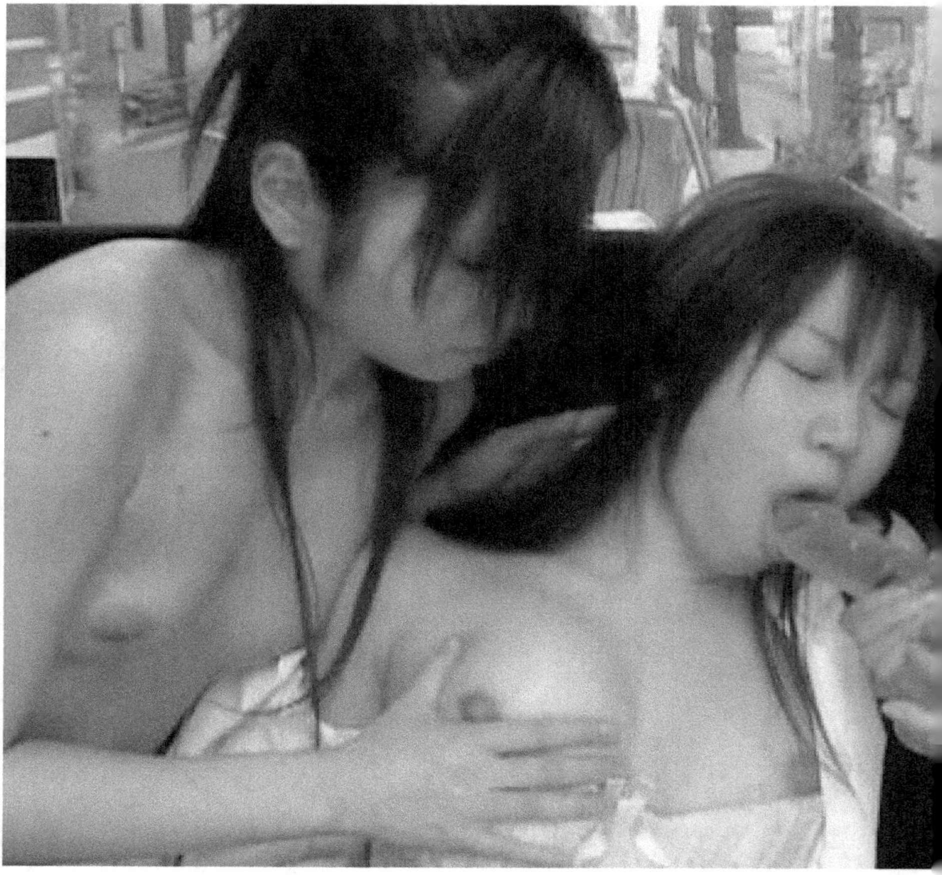

The above portrayed mind-blowing and mouth-watering
enchantingly elegant photograph of these two unspoil
virgin cuties exposing their depilated straight-line vagina
marks the end of this rare Pictorial Analysis